THE COMPOSITION COMMONS

THE COMPOSITION COMMONS

Writing a New Idea of the University

JESSICA YOOD

UTAH STATE UNIVERSITY PRESS
Logan

© 2024 by University Press of Colorado

Published by Utah State University Press
An imprint of University Press of Colorado
1580 North Logan Street, Suite 660
PMB 39883
Denver, Colorado 80203-1942

 The University Press of Colorado is a proud member of
the Association of University Presses.

The University Press of Colorado is a cooperative publishing enterprise supported, in part, by Adams State University, Colorado State University, Fort Lewis College, Metropolitan State University of Denver, University of Alaska Fairbanks, University of Colorado, University of Denver, University of Northern Colorado, University of Wyoming, Utah State University, and Western Colorado University.

∞ This paper meets the requirements of the ANSI/NISO Z39.48-1992 (Permanence of Paper).

ISBN: 978-1-64642-541-9 (hardcover)
ISBN: 978-1-64642-542-6 (paperback)
ISBN: 978-1-64642-543-3 (ebook)
https://doi.org/10.7330/9781646425433

Library of Congress Cataloging-in-Publication Data
Names: Yood, Jessica, author.
Title: The composition commons : writing a new idea of the university / Jessica Yood.
Description: Logan : Utah State University Press, [2024] | Includes bibliographical references and index.
Identifiers: LCCN 2023032327 (print) | LCCN 2023032328 (ebook) | ISBN 9781646425419 (hardcover) | ISBN 9781646425426 (paperback) | ISBN 9781646425433 (ebook)
Subjects: LCSH: Herbert H. Lehman College. | English language—Composition and exercises—Study and teaching (Higher) | English language—Rhetoric—Study and teaching (Higher) | English language—Writing—Study and teaching (Higher) | Literacy—Study and teaching (Higher)—Research. | College students' writings, American—New York (State)—New York—Evaluation. | College students' writings, American—New York (State)—New York—Case studies.
Classification: LCC PE1404 .Y66 2024 (print) | LCC PE1404 (ebook) | DDC 428.0071—dc23/eng/20231204
LC record available at https://lccn.loc.gov/2023032327
LC ebook record available at https://lccn.loc.gov/2023032328

Cover photographs: (top) iStock/shapecharge; (bottom) aerial photograph of Lehman College campus Speech and Music Building with APEX in the background. © 2023, Lehman College. Used with permission.

To
Avi and Leo, Gabriel, Dahlia

For
David Saul Yood

CONTENTS

ACKNOWLEDGMENTS

I am profoundly grateful to students and colleagues at Lehman College and the Graduate Center of the City University of New York, my intellectual home for over two decades. The undergraduates named and referenced in this book, and so many Lehman and GC students, were and are invaluable to my work and life. My collaborators in the Writing Across the Curriculum program gave me lasting lessons on putting ideas into practice. Thank you to innovators Sondra Perl and Marcie Wolfe and to the greater cohort: Mark McBeth, Tyler T. Schmidt, Robyn Spencer, Alyshia Gálvez, Dhipinder Walia, Vani Kannan, Sophia Hsu, Michelle Augustine, Olivia Loksing Moy, Bret Maney, Sarah Soanirina Ohmer, Elaine Avidon, Linda Hirsch, Peter Gray, Kultej Dhariwal, Gabrielle Kappes, Amy J. Wan, Todd Craig, and the late, sorely missed Cindy Lobel.

This work benefited from several grants, especially the Mellon Transformative Learning in the Humanities fellowship, and from every faculty member in the excellent Lehman and GC English departments. Department directors and deans lent support when I needed it. Thank you Paula Loscocco, Mario DiGangi, and Marcie Wolfe (again), Mark McBeth (again), Walter Blanco, David Hyman, Siraj Ahmed, Karin Beck, Rene Parmar, and James Mahon. Admiration and appreciation for Kandice Chuh, who gave existential encouragement and profound, on-point feedback.

There are not enough words (both would advise brevity anyway) to adequately thank Deirdre O'Boy and Tyler T. Schmidt. Deirdre allowed me access to her teaching and her insatiable intelligence and wit. Tyler treated very rough drafts with tenderness and his usual terrific insight.

Thank you to Rachael Levay, the team at USUP, and the two peer reviewers, who challenged and motivated me. Crossing paths with these colleagues made my work better: thank you Neisha-Anne Green and Leonard Cassuto, Kurt Spellmeyer, Deborah Holdstein, David

Bleich, Julie Jung, Mary McKinney, Tamara K. Nopper, Stacey Olster, Ira Livingston, Carmen Kynard, Lisa Blankenship, John Rufo, and Selin Kalostyan. Fabulous librarians with Stanford University's Special Collections and at Lehman College assisted with the archival study. Heidi Johnsen's take on this (on most things) was just right. Pat Belanoff has been a mentor and role model for much of my adult life; I hope this honors some of her brilliant, expansive spirit.

The communities I belong to in and around Riverdale, dear friends and partners in parenting, buoyed me. Lori Kurlander and the Kurlander family, Rona Sheramy, and Adam Segal offered fresh perspectives and helped in other ways too, as did long-time confidant Diana Holm, and Yael Slonim and the Commack crew.

Family deserves more than I can manage here. Thank you to my first, fiercest reader, my late grandfather Leo Vine, and to the Daniels, Alan Yood and Maria Russo, Brenda and Jerry Deener, the Vines, and the Deener-Agus and Deener-Chodirker clan. My parents, Nora and Barry Yood, and my sister, Marla Yood Daniels, believed in me. My mother taught me to love literature, seek justice, and swim. Marla knows a lot and also why this—why everything—is infused with the memory of our beloved brother and best friend, David Saul Yood.

I dedicate this to Avi Deener and to our children. Leo, Gabriel, and Dahlia helped me grow into my writing life even as they did a lot of growing up of their own, becoming the incredible young adults they are now. Without the unconditional support and love of my husband I could not have taken on this project. But it is the project of our shared life that matters most, and it is Avi who understands this most of all.

THE COMPOSITION COMMONS

Introduction

WRITING A NEW IDEA OF THE UNIVERSITY

This book, about the power of ordinary, collective composition practices, took shape in a place of unparalleled isolation and under extraordinary circumstances. The global Covid-19 pandemic was still ravaging New York City when I rode an empty city bus four miles from home to my college campus. I went to revisit data from a research project completed a few years earlier. Institutional Review Board (IRB) protocols forbade me from removing the "human subject" material—hundreds of pages of student writing produced in two composition classes—locked in a file cabinet in the Writing Across the Curriculum (WAC) office at Lehman College, one of the City University of New York (CUNY) schools and where I teach. The freewrites and letters I had collated and coded in 2012 and 2013 are part of an archive used to assess the efficacy of what had been an historic new curriculum at my institution. "Pathways," the first general education reform at CUNY in half a century, was also the first curriculum to institute university-wide standards for composition courses. The new courses were mandated in 2011 and piloted in 2012. We were coming close to its tenth anniversary. I figured I'd spend the lockdown doing a follow-up report.

It was a gray day at the end of October of 2020. The local Bronx bus made one stop, in front of my son's high school, which had become the site of an Army Corps of Engineers Covid-19 testing center. The driver looked askance when I motioned through the plastic barrier that I needed to go two more blocks, to the college. I got off the bus and found the gates boarded up and blocked by a tarp tent, where a public safety officer sat. He checked my one-day pass through a window the size of my faculty ID. I made it across the campus and to the English department on the third floor of Carman Hall without passing a single person. When I unlocked the door to the WAC office, I found six chairs pulled out inches from the seminar table, as if its occupants had stepped out for a moment and not seven months. I avoided the chairs and settled for the floor. My posture was the same as sitting Shiva, a ritual I know too

https://doi.org/10.7330/9781646425433.c000

well. In Jewish practice, the mourner lowers herself to receive visitors, a reminder that loss reorients everything.

Of course no one was coming to visit Lehman, or the several high schools within a few blocks of campus. We were nearly a year into the pandemic and without a clear plan for teaching the city's students. New York City has the largest public school system in the nation, and CUNY is the country's largest urban public university. The relationship between the two is intimate. Most CUNY students attended a city high school, undergraduates are often caregivers for school-aged kids, and graduate students work as staff or faculty in the districts. Among those in the field of composition and rhetoric, the connection between K–12 and CUNY goes back decades, to the days of open admissions, Basic Writing, and the birth of the New York City Writing Project. In the summer of 2020, many of us with ties to both systems joined leaders in advocacy groups to support students and staff working in the most challenging of situations. We organized book swaps and drop-off sites for free lunch access, delivered computers and set up Wi-Fi for families in shelters and other compromised housing situations, connected tutors to kids with learning differences, and created caregiver support networks.

But by late September, with no definitive word about reopening or improved remote options, we started to lose hope. Every week, more students stopped attending classes. The Covid cases would go up in the schools, the buildings would close, and the supply chain for resources stalled. The frustration and injustice of it all motivated us one week and left us listless the next. For many, distance learning just wasn't going to work. For many community organizers, remote advocacy barely scratched the surface of need.

Exasperation and exhaustion summed up my home situation too. My family felt crowded yet deeply alone in the private ways we were falling apart. For five years, my husband had lived with a complicated but manageable disease. Now we were paralyzed with fear about his "underlying condition." That led to draconian rules for our three kids. The oldest rebelled, contracted the virus, then retreated completely. Our middle child lost the majority of services he received for a language disability, and with them, much of his enthusiasm for learning. The youngest went into school, but Covid outbreaks sent kids home for weeks at a time. Each quarantine period convinced her that it was best to stay put. She'd join me most afternoons in the bedroom, lying under the covers and out of view of the laptop camera while I taught. We'd wait out the days like this, autumn's diminishing light daring us to do it again tomorrow.

Still we were doing better than many. By spring of 2020 the Bronx had become what the *New York Times* called a "virus hotspot."[1] In this poorest borough of New York City, Lehman is the only public four-year college. We knew then, and now have data proving, that working-class communities and people of color have been the hardest hit from the pandemic. A Hispanic Serving Institution, Lehman's population is around 80 percent Latinx or Black, majority women, and more than half the students come from homes making under $30,000 a year.[2] Scholars have predicted that when the final tallies come in, CUNY students, staff, and faculty will have suffered the most sickness and death of any university in the country.[3]

A snapshot of my 2020–2021 courses provides some specifics. Of the eighty-five undergraduates in my classes, all said they wanted to be back on campus and all agreed this would "never or not for a long time" happen. Twenty-six had dropped one or more of their classes since March 2020. This included a nurse who was in her last year of school, having returned at age forty-three to become an English teacher. Two mothers around my age had waited a combined nineteen years to enroll in college. They didn't return in September. More than half of my students logged on to borrowed computers from apartment hallways, parked cars, or a semiprivate place in the following workspaces: Starbucks, hospitals, nursing homes, daycare centers, UPS trucks, restaurant kitchens, and subway stations. Thirty-seven students said they shared a room with family members who were also learning remotely. Some days just a handful of students showed up to our Zoom meetings, apologizing because they couldn't stay for the entire class. A few would message me during class to describe a dangerous job or a death in the family. I tried to manage the private chat, filled with personal despair, while maintaining morale. I'd revamp lessons, reach out to individual students, rally the group with a playlist, a podcast, or just a video of strangers jostling for seats on crowded subway cars. Sometimes this fell flat and I sounded like the ringleader in some ridiculous ruse. Other times, everyone got in on the act, sharing photos or posting poignant passages from assigned reading. These days lifted spirits, but never for long.

Longing and an urgency to connect: that's how I felt but not what I told the dean when I sought special permission to be on campus. "Return to research" was the subject heading of a desperate email sent to senior administration. The college could use an updated analysis of general education and a retrospective look at outcomes for composition, my email stated. If I could just get to those old files, I explained, I'd reevaluate the data, check it against new research and disciplinary-specific reforms, and write a new curricular report.

The report never happened. Instead I spent the rest of that October and then the next three years rereading the artifacts from these Lehman College English 111 courses and from student writing produced in classrooms just like them. Reading the texts in relationship to each other revealed this material resonating with a rapidly changed context, the one we live in now. The samples spoke to me and to the way classroom writing pursues a shared space of collective practice and connected learning. I call that space the composition commons.

Engaging in archives from two pivotal moments in history—the late 1930s, at the start of the general education movement, and the early 2000s, when a diverse, nontraditional student demographic demands that we reconsider common learning—*The Composition Commons* traces the epistemological properties and social powers of informal classroom writing, tracks how it creates a new idea of the university, and argues that we center this idea in the academy.

METHODOLOGY, 2012–2018: RESEARCHING REFORM

I did not set out to write a book about an idea of the university. My research began, like many writing studies projects do, with an attempt to understand and reform classroom outcomes, curricular goals, and pedagogy. In 2012 and 2013, I was one of the writing program administrators charged with enacting Pathways, the new general education curriculum, for the first-year writing classes at Lehman. The primary purpose of Pathways was to ease the transfer process so students could more seamlessly go from two-year to four-year schools and streamline their time earning a degree. This local goal, particular to the demographics at CUNY, was described as part of a national agenda to transform higher education. Administrators pointed to places "like Harvard" that had initiated general education reforms of their own to ready students for what the board of trustees called the "knowledge needed . . . in a new century."[4] That phrase, and the reference to elite institutions, came up in glossy brochures and a promotional blitz sent to faculty, students, and the media. The materials described why a bold, standardized new "common core" would "update" CUNY for a new era.[5]

As college writing programs adopted this new general education curriculum, many also sought new assessments. In 2012, several Lehman composition courses became part of a pilot project study that would lead to adopting the Written Communication VALUES Rubric of the American Association of Colleges and Universities (AAC&U). About a dozen sections of English 111, the first of our two required writing courses, would measure one central competency listed among the Pathways composition outcomes: the ability to compose "well-constructed essays that develop clearly defined aims, that are supported by close, textual reading."[6] The AAC&U rubric would evaluate this skill using three high-stakes student essays: a narrative and two academic arguments.

Lehman's WAC program had used the AAC&U rubric before, and I knew it wouldn't capture the many discourses of the composition course.[7] So as part of a sabbatical research project, I secured IRB permission to investigate the range of writing happening in the new curriculum. I enrolled in two semesters of English 111, did the work, got a grade, and gathered hundreds of artifacts.[8] My central research question was simple: how do students talk about the writing they're asked to do in the new curriculum?[9]

Over two years, I collected 232 writing samples from forty-five students enrolled in English 111. My methodology drew from autoethnographic classroom studies and case study research. Suresh A. Canagarajah suggests that autoethnography enables knowledge to develop "without depending on researchers from the center" (2012, 117). Multilingual students and scholars and others from the margins of the academy can find this type of research "friendly," he argues, because lived literacy experiences of all kinds, and not only those that echo existing literature, are relevant. Guided by Canagarajah's literacy studies, I took a reflective stance to the data, focusing on formal and informal writing and listening and recording classroom interactions. I chose two sections taught by "Prof D," as she preferred to be called. I knew the instructor professionally but not very well. She was experienced, recently tenured as a full-time lecturer, and one of the instructors piloting the AAC&U rubric to evaluate student writing.

Between 2014 and 2015, a year after I completed the classroom research, I used the AAC&U Rubric as a model to code the writing produced in two English 111 sections. My research assistants and I recorded each time students named the genres required or the five learning outcomes provided in the rubric.[10]

The study revealed that students rarely referred to the genres required for the formal essays, though these were described in the Pathways outcomes, in the course syllabus, and in the particular assignment prompts. Even when students were asked to write a letter or compose a freewrite specifically about their arguments and narratives, their texts seldom mentioned these assignments as such. The learning outcomes were sometimes touched on, but not often. On the other hand, students named the work they saw happening in freewrites and letters. There could be many reasons why students refrained from discussing certain assignments. My colleagues and I decided to avoid conjecture and focus on what the freewriting and letters didn't do: reveal much about genre and outcomes in general education composition courses.

After months of coding, WAC coordinators and I drew on this data to create a new professional development agenda for general education and composition. We determined that the curriculum should focus more on how students "transfer" their writing knowledge from course to course and school to school. Transfer, an important "threshold concept" in the field of writing studies, seemed critical to the success of Pathways. We used the informal texts in the archive, combined with the data collected in the rubrics, to track "background knowledge"—information, knowledge, skills, and content students possess when they come to college. This helped us understand what students might need in composition and beyond. We agreed with writing scholars who found that when students learn for transfer, they "draw upon, use, and repurpose" prior writing skills and knowledge and achieve success in "new settings" (Robertson, Taczak, and Yancey 2012). Over the next few years, we revamped WAC workshops, and in 2018, my college revised assessment guidelines for first-year composition, published collaborative studies on pedagogy, and developed curricular guides for departments.[11]

METHODOLOGY, 2020–2022: FROM RESEARCHING REFORM TO RENDERING A COMMONS

The original purpose of my study was to investigate how student writing realizes the aims of a curricular reform. But when I encountered the archive again, in a city shut down by a pandemic and a campus silenced by the absence of students, that curriculum faded into the background. In this altered reality, I discovered other patterns in the language, other knowledge forms.

Most noticeably, the freewriting and letters no longer represented something that might "transfer" from one situation to another. Rather the artifacts were tethering me to this place, this moment, telling me about ways that classroom writing brings people and ideas together, whether physically with each other or not. I heard conversations between student and student and between student and the academy that pulsated with presence, purpose, and sustained spirit. Instead of certainties about reform, these artifacts spoke to how ordinary students make connections in and across time, write to belong somewhere, and render knowledge in the common pursuit of practice. By the end of 2021, a new question about composition was starting to form. How does knowledge formed in one time and in another place transfer to a world in the process of becoming something else?

This question guided another kind of archival analysis. Anthropologist Elizabeth Chin's 2016 *My Life with Things* offered a model for rethinking artifacts over time and in time. Chin's unusual ethnography is part diary of personal consumer habits, part reflections on those habits, and part ideological critique of mass consumerism in late capitalism. Over many years, she wrote field notes of her consumption habits and also watched how those notes read differently as the objects she purchased served different uses. After data collection, she deviated from the more systematic ethnographic recordkeeping and wrote self-contained essays, in a single setting, in an attempt to perform some rigorous work of memory.

My approach to collecting and analyzing the data from English 111 was similar. As an enrolled student, I took field notes from the two English 111 classes, reflected on classroom practices as I participated, and recorded student observations and my own, but did not look at the student writing until the semester concluded. Only months and years after that, when I was trying to do one thing—describe a curriculum—did I end up doing something else: describing an idea of the university.

For this next round of artifact coding, I relied on an approach to literacy research adopted from Deborah Brandt. Brandt explains how everyday informal accounts matter to how we track large-scale literacy developments. Her research documents one major literacy change in the twenty-first century, that we are "becoming a nation of authors" (qtd. in Plante 2018). These new authors are "witnesses to socio-historical processes, witnesses who can report out from their particular locations in place and time and social structure" (Brandt 2021, 263). During 2020 and 2021, I analyzed the student samples and considered these writers as witnesses and authors. I adopted a "grounded theory" methodology, noting what Brandt calls "mentions," or "discrete verbal references to events, processes, actions, facts, presumptions that pertain to the phenomena of interest" (2021, 268).[12]

Over a year's time, I observed when "mentions" did not resonate with the curricular outcomes, but did with each other. I started listing the phrases repeated over and over, coming from a time and place of the past but also speaking to me and to each other in the present. I followed Brandt's lead in presenting the accounts of everyday persons as critical matter for literacy and cultural studies. Attending to the writing of "non-elite people whose voices are usually absent from official representations," my analysis of individual student artifacts is not meant to be representative of particular identity groups but instead illuminate systemic patterns in collections of discourse (Brandt 2021, 263). I checked the patterns that I found with other educators and spent a year doing "wide background reading" or "sensitizing" (Brandt 2021, 266). My reading stretched back a century. I found the contents of that one file cabinet resonating with the contents of dozens of other file cabinets of classroom material, and with a dynamic story about student writing and higher education in America. The artifacts came together to form a tradition that transcends curricular reforms and even global pandemics. This is a tradition of students composing an academic commons.

HISTORY AND IDEA OF THE ACADEMIC COMMONS

The *academic commons* as I define it is a social collective generated by writing practices that happen in the classrooms of public, nonprestigious colleges and universities. This material does not invent the commons. Rather the commons is enacted, again and again, *by* the artifacts, as they are made, classroom by classroom, practice by writing practice.

Although this project focuses on writing practices and classrooms, *the commons* is not a term I take from the field of composition studies. *Commons* is a term that resists ownership. It means the collectives that form in a particular time and place, and among persons working together, but it does not belong to a single period, region, or intellectual tradition. A commons is a living entity, contingent on the material contributions and gathering of human endeavors. One cannot define *commons* without calling attention to activities making those things.

The historical definition of the commons goes back to medieval Europe, where a commons referred to particular land farmed on by commoners, or people without power in the aristocracy, church, or related hierarchies. Today, we think of the commons as anything we do as a group, in an enclosed area of collective engagement. For example, Lehman College has a dining commons, a coffee shop and food court where students and faculty meet and eat together. I am one of the many bloggers published on a digital commons, a shared space for CUNY-affiliated students and teachers. Several colleagues helped create a green space commons at Lehman and in nearby areas of the Bronx, an edible garden cultivated for campus members and surrounding communities.[13]

As these examples illustrate, my university has adopted the term *commons* to describe communal social justice projects. But the commons has not always been conjured for the benefit of members of the public whose work I study here, students and teachers who are mostly women of color, work full- or nearly full-time, commute, and have significant caretaking responsibilities. Indeed, we cannot separate "commons" from its counterpart, "enclosure," a strategy whereby the powerful determine the value of the resources and activities of those without power or status (Kamola and Meyerhoff 2009). Enclosure policies have their roots in settler colonialism and policies that restricted, suppressed, or violently eradicated the lives, lands, literacies, and institutions of many of the educators and students discussed in the chapters that follow. For example, Craig Steven Wilder's *Ebony and Ivy* details how the first colleges in this country, constructed to benefit democracy and promote enlightened politics, were built using enslaved labor and on Indigenous land. The Morrill Land-Grant Act of 1862 also sought a shared good through education. This act can be traced to increased access to schooling for poor and rural areas of America. Yet it also enabled the federal government to occupy land and then create institutions where the original inhabitants of that land would be excluded from admissions (Stein 2018). Closer to home, it's easy to document examples of educational policies and curricular reforms directed at the general public that end up restricting or policing freedoms for specific groups. In the late 1990s, my university's board of trustees began a campaign that would "return" CUNY to its history of "excellence" so that it could be a resource for the good of the city. By 2000, a set of austerity measures and new admissions procedures effectively closed what was left of open-admissions programming at CUNY's four-year schools. In the early 2000s, literacy initiatives, like SEEK (Search for Education, Elevation, and Knowledge), so critical to innovative research and teaching in composition, and so important to my own pedagogical growth, were moved out of colleges like my own. SEEK served English Language Learners and poor students who needed support to start their degrees. In this case, what was called a "public good" became more exclusionary, limiting learning options for the increasingly multilingual and Black and Brown population attending CUNY in the twenty-first century.[14]

Given this history and the often corrupt use of the commons, it's no wonder that many books like mine, about literacy and public education, avoid abstract ideas and stick to concrete concerns of persons and institutions. Ideas take us into metaphysics and spirituality. Classroom writing practices confront the here and now. There are tensions that rise to the surface whenever we situate local, specific literacy practices alongside abstract concepts. Throughout this book we explore these tensions. In fact we celebrate them as critical to building a new idea of a university in the practices of a public academy.

This is a different idea of a university than Cardinal John Henry Newman posited when he coined the phrase in 1852. When he first delivered his famous book *The Idea of a University* as a series of lectures, Newman was on a mission to make the academy a sacred space, to sanctify it with higher concerns. College should take students away from the tensions of the day, giving them a home to seek communion with a higher purpose. Knowledge is bigger than the self, and the self has a soul connected to a pure intellectual spirit. A "gentleman" forms when released from the confines of the day-to-day, when he learns transcendent, timeless truths; this enables him to join a "civilization" of intellects. And for Newman, intellect and civilization emerge in harmony with literature and great humanistic works. Through engagement with the liberal arts, an "ideal" is realized: universal knowledge formed in "mutual dependence" (Newman 1996, 221, 99).

Mutual dependence laced with individual liberation: this is an idea with lasting appeal. Indeed, *The Idea of a University* has been traced to major educational movements of the last century (Turner 1996). General education curricula, ubiquitous in American colleges and universities, is one place where we can see the influence. Historians talk about this American invention as the twentieth-century enactment of Newman's nineteenth-century vision. Credit for remaking this ideal into curriculum goes to a few descendants of Newman's, humanists who created the liberal education requirement at elite institutions like the University of Chicago, Columbia, and Harvard. Out of these early-twentieth-century "common learnings" programs came a post–World War II commitment to reform, next an investment in literary studies as a core subject, and finally the adoption of general education curricula as the nation's conduit to the commons. The goal of this kind of commons education was to release students from what one postwar manifesto called the "the stranglehold of the present" (Harvard Committee 1945, 70).

Of course the present found its way into Harvard's curriculum and into all of academia, including core courses. The concerns of the present prompted dissent, critique, and continued revision of common learnings. Yet even as we alter what liberal education means and which books count as great, a reading-centered idea of the university maintains a hold on the national conversation, even in this post-pandemic era of change. The continued influence of an idea of the university generated at these prestige places carries on because, as Louis Menand writes, "historically, the elites have had the resources to innovate and the visibility to set standards for the system as a whole" (2010, 18).

My book, written from the perspective of a compositionist at a nonprestige public college, presents a rebuttal to the belief that selective universities are the sole engines of innovation in the academy. I join with others who argue that if "historically" elite institutions get the resources, then we need to uncover undervalued contributions of marginalized institutions and fight for reallocation of funding.[15] Yet here I make an additional claim. We need to define resources differently, not in terms of artifacts of the elite or abstract reforms detached from the lives of students and destined to become commodities, but as composing practices. The university can still be a liberating space. Yet it does not liberate *from* but *in* the confrontation and connection of the here and now. *The Composition Commons* conjures this idea of liberal education by telling the story of how students author a new kind of academic commons for this changing world.

AUTHORS AND MATERIALS OF THE ACADEMIC COMMONS

We are not accustomed to thinking of undergraduates as authoring an idea of the university because we are not accustomed to seeing student writing as cultural material. Yet investigating neglected places and practices leads us to some inventive epistemologies. That is an idea of the university I take from public commons advocates who animate this book. The first woman to win the Nobel Prize in Economics, Elinor Ostrom, is one pioneer of a practice-based commons. Ostrom articulates the commons as a big concept often enacted in small activities and overlooked areas. Her work refuted an earlier understanding of the commons, ecologist Garrett Hardin's 1968 conclusion that the "tragedy of the commons" is society's inability to manage resources. Hardin's essay argued that land must be owned and enclosed, monitored from above and privatized, to avoid overuse and unequal distribution. Ostrom's 1990 counterthesis, *Governing the Commons: The Evolution of Institutions for Collective Action*, documented economic and environmentally sustainable possibilities in farming collectives. Later in her career, Ostrom extended her study of commoning beyond agricultural communities and joined with international scholars to define the "knowledge commons." Along with Charlotte Hess, Ostrom defined the knowledge commons as an ongoing, ecological process that expands access by always requiring the search for new sources and new archives (Hess and Ostrom 2006). These approaches to research also broaden our notion of what and who makes knowledge and shapes social life.

The classroom activities that I count as part of the knowledge commons have been described as "vernacular" communicative practices. In her *Commons Democracy*, Dana D. Nelson (2015) uses the term *vernacular* to describe "immediate, informal, and non-delegable" practices depicted in pre–Revolutionary War novels of early America (7). Because we rely on official documents created by the leading figures of history, our conception of shared governance is bound up with the legacy of war and the theories of representative politics that became national lore. Nelson invokes commoning literary practices as articulating additional and alternative values of democracy. Carmen Kynard's *Vernacular Insurrections*, about the literacy interventions of the Black Freedom movement, broadens the meaning of vernacular beyond "local" uses of a community's everyday language. Her study reveals the critical contribution Black literacy activists have made to American history and to writing studies. These vernacular practices don't just chip away at the dominant culture but remake it (2014, 11).

Critics Kandice Chuh and Roderick A. Ferguson also turn to alternative "humanisms and humanities" for claiming a commons (Chuh 2019, 24). These humanisms locate "roots" of culture that are "undisciplined" and invent new "modes of intellection and institutionality" (Ferguson 2021, 76). Their studies of African American and Asian American literatures show how our understanding of history, politics, culture, and aesthetics changes when we encounter texts different from the Eurocentric norm of Western culture. Drawing on philosopher Pierre Dardot and sociologist Christian Laval, as well as evidence on rising global inequities, compositionist James Rushing Daniel's 2022 *Toward an Anti-Capitalist Composition* offers examples of affirmative, justice-oriented "common" pedagogies that resist "the divisive and destructive project of capitalist accumulation" (25).

Resisting accumulation as an ethos defines the project of many new histories of the academy, including la paperson's 2017 *A Third University Is Possible*. This polemic turns back to pivotal moments in higher education, and specifically to the origin of land-grant colleges in America created after the Morrill Acts of 1862 and 1890. Indigenous Americans and Black Americans were displaced by these policies and communities continue to live with the consequences. Yet there is energy, activism, intellectual innovation, and camaraderie happening here. La paperson draws from third-world feminists who recognize where transformation in community and politics occurs, even in colonizing spaces. A third-world university commits to this kind of transformation as it happens in local movements and in "scrap material" made in parts, over time; this is an idea of the university already underway, it "already exists" (la paperson 2017, 43, 52). Liberation through learning is an aspiration and an urgent reality of spaces ignored or injured by official policy.

Like Chuh, Ferguson, Daniel, and la paperson, this book looks for "modes of intellect and institution" in scrap parts and local movements, in roots and forms of resistance ignored or hidden in plain sight. But unlike the literary texts, political papers, or public pedagogies centered in their projects, my book focuses on informal texts composed by individual students writing together in classrooms. We don't always define this material by its change-making features. By "we" I mean those of us in writing studies, who spend a lot of time with undergraduate composition, but not usually to mine ideas on transforming the academy. I also mean historians of higher education and cultural critics who care deeply about the university but rarely see low-stakes writing produced in introductory courses as resources for research. I argue that we must look again at these practices and their authors as forming a new academic commons.

The particular materials centered here are freewriting and reflective letters. They will be familiar to many, but I aim to defamiliarize them. Freewriting is known as the practice of writing about anything, nonstop, for a certain amount of time. Peter Elbow (2012), the scholar most associated with freewriting, calls it a heuristic to use our "vernacular" or to speak "on the page" (395). Reflective letters or "cover letters" are often what Kathleen Blake Yancey (1998) calls "first-person" accounts composed after finishing an assignment (26).

One way to see these practices anew is to treat them as genres or "typified rhetorical actions based in recurrent situations" (Miller 1984, 159). Carolyn Miller claims genres as "cultural artifacts." I take Miller's "invitation" to focus on student writing as "an anthropologist sees a material artifact" with "patterns" that are "interrelated" (Miller 1994, 69). To trace the interrelated patterns in the informal student writing of classroom artifacts across time and space, I rely on an extensive body of research in rhetorical genre studies and critical pedagogy. I pay attention to what students said about the freewriting and letters to consider the features of genres "hidden" from the public because they are considered private or confidential (Devitt 2016, 14). Neither public nor private, freewriting and letter writing are "complex performances that take place in-between and around" recognizable discourses (Reiff and Bawarshi 2016, 188). They provide insight that official genres of the university—curricular reforms, disciplinary paradigms, scholarly manifestos—often obscure.

Three features of these genres guided my decision to center these practices. First, they are prevalent practices in classrooms and can be taken up today, and indeed, they were the most common writing activities observed in all the archives I studied. Second, these writing practices have a unique place in the history of general education in America. Most writing scholars trace these genres to the 1970s-era pioneering research of process paradigm compositionists; however, I uncover an earlier and more commons-oriented use of these practices. Third, of all the informal writing I studied, these were the two genres that prompted shared learning.

Freewriting and reflective letters are widely known but by no means universally used in college courses. Some access these activities as writers and teachers but wouldn't consider them suitable for creating an academic commons. Others might find these practices, especially their print-based forms, irrelevant to communication and knowledge-making in the digital age. In my own writing classes, I encourage public-facing genres, such as podcasts, blogs, and zines. Certainly these forms of writing can contribute to a commons. However, my research discovered that freewriting and reflective letters have a unique role to play in crafting shared knowledge. Freewriting and reflective letters straddle the line between home and school, job and course, campus and street, and reveal tensions and explore the invention of knowledges that happen on the border of our composing worlds. They highlight individual background knowledges and situate these knowledges in the content of the course. They direct readers to attend to students as authors. And they reflect on the state of the university and on the place of students in composing content for the academic commons.

OVERVIEW OF *THE COMPOSITION COMMONS*

That the university can be a commons is an old idea. That ordinary composition practices produced in nonelitist public college classrooms can create a commons is an idea to embrace now, as we face a new era in higher education. When ordinary persons go to college, they are labeled "nontraditional" and the schools they attend "nonselective." The nontraditional are older than twenty, working, have dependents or substantial family responsibilities, take "uneven" paths to degrees, often are first-generation, and commute. Increasingly, these students are also recent immigrants, speakers of more than one language, people of color, and women. For most of American history, this demographic was the minority enrolled in higher education. Today the nontraditional is the typical student who attends Lehman college. And they are the typical undergraduates in this country, making up the new academic majority.[16]

These students, and all Americans who have attended postsecondary schools over the last half-century, have two experiences in common: taking a required composition course and completing some form of general education requirement, both mandatory at over 80 percent of American colleges and universities.[17] Debate about the value of these courses is as ubiquitous now as it was in the 1870s and 1880s, when composition was invented, and in the 1940s, when general education programs became commonplace. But there is little debate that writing occupies much of our time and energy. Like all of us, these undergraduates are writing more than ever, composing in multiple, informal ways as part of class and while in classrooms, in a variety of contexts and in combinations of modalities, moving from screen to scrap of paper to social media countless times. What do we know about how this new academic majority gathers in writing and how their practices might transform higher learning in America? By the end of this book, I aim to answer this question.

The first half of *The Composition Commons* uses historical research to uncover the origins of the composition commons as an idea of the university. I track this idea to a forgotten nationwide writing-based general education project, the Stanford Language Arts Investigation (SLAI). From 1937 to 1940, this three-year integrated language arts experiment piloted courses for ten thousand public school and college students, with the goal of centering informal student writing, especially freewriting and reflective letters, what the SLAI called "contact" composition and "reconstructive" genres. Chapter 1 explores four monographs and thousands of pages of student writing and teacher ethnographies culled from the archives of the SLAI. I detail the practices of the two hundred language arts classes taught in what were then "new" public schools built for workers, adults, recent immigrants, and the poor.

This history revisits well-known architects of general education like philosopher John Dewey and literary critic I. A. Richards. I contrast their views with lesser-known public school and college educators. We meet Louise Noyes and Alvina Treut Burrows, compositionists who forwarded "contact composition" as a genre of the commons, and Charlemae Hill Rollins, editor of the National Council of Teachers of English (NCTE) inaugural anthology of African American writings, who championed reflective writing or "lived-in" letters. Such practices contributed to a public school–centered, anti-racist, "reconstructive" vision for education, a radical alternative to the top-down liberal arts agenda of the day. That alternative vision erodes in the post-war years, as general education becomes a national agenda and the composition commons idea of the university is deserted. As chapter 2 explains, Harvard's influential 1945 report *General Education in a Free Society* codified the commons as the "close" study of "heritage texts" for the purpose of national "cultural literacy." The chapter describes the long shadow cast by cultural literacy, influencing the late-twentieth-century culture wars, the adoption of the Common Core State Standards in the early twenty-first century, and the post-Covid-19 calls to reinstate "liberal education" as a solution to global crisis.

The differences between general education, with its reading commons idea of the university, and the SLAI with its composition commons idea of the university, are stark. General education asserts reading as the tool for, and representation of, shared background knowledge. The SLAI positioned composition practices as a source for creating shared knowledge. Liberal education emerged in great books courses at elite universities, and the SLAI took place in public high schools and public colleges and forwarded nontraditional students as authors of cultural material. The SLAI, disqualified from general education curricula and erased from history, is the model I draw from to revive the composition commons today.

The second half of the book offers offer two case studies of contact and reconstructive practices as they unfold in today's college courses. Attention to these practices reorients what we think the American academy was, where its innovations happen, and who can be the authors we turn to for a new idea of the university. Here we meet students in contemporary composition classes at Lehman College, CUNY, who carry on the tradition of the Stanford Language Arts Investigation. In chapter 3, we are introduced to Xavier, an adult student in English 111 who invented a new vocabulary for freewriting. His work, along with the other student artifacts, casts a different light on course content, liberal education, and intellectual history. Their contact compositions challenge commonplace understanding of what background knowledge is and how it's used in the "transfer" of knowledge and skills. Chapter 4 begins with a letter written by the Latinx Student Alliance at Lehman College about the need for diversity in English courses and explores the role of letters in challenging curricular updates. Inspired by SLAI teacher-researchers, who argued that student correspondences are investments in "reconstructive" communication, the chapter describes features of student letters that redefine diversity, equity, and inclusion. These letters echo the arguments of mobility and genre scholars, feminist rhetors, and critical pedagogues, who articulate the limitations of reform. In reading the correspondence of student writers we find actualization of these arguments. They are in the lived epistemological practices that matter in the academy.

Not all informal writing can produce a commons. And not everyone will agree that shared knowledge is possible or that college classrooms are the places to go looking for it. There is ample cause for cynicism about writing programs and for the future of public higher education. But this book is not primarily a critique. A substantial scholarly canon already exists to chronicle crisis. What we need now are new forms of contact and belonging, new approaches to reconstruct the academy. It is to these forms and approaches we turn now, as we recover and reclaim the composition commons for the university.

1

READING TO REFORM, WRITING TO FORM A WORLD SOCIETY, 1937–1945

For nearly a century, we've looked to reading to render an academic commons. The relationship between the books assigned in college and how we cultivate shared learning is what I call the "reading commons" idea of the university. This idea gained ground when general education became a curricular staple of the American academy. In the early part of the twentieth century, the pursuit of an academic commons was a minor concern. By the 1930s, a newly urgent conversation about national identity in a democracy erupted, centered on liberal arts courses. After World War II, following an influx of federal funding and policies that dramatically expanded access to higher learning, general education curricula flourished. At that point, humanities, and their common core reading lists, came to define general education in America.

Today, almost all colleges and universities require some kind of general education program; these classes account for one-third of the courses taken by undergraduates (Wells 2016). At my own university, the general education program is described as the heart of the institution. The City University of New York has twenty-five very different kinds of college campuses across five boroughs. Its general education initiative, "Pathways," binds them all, providing a practical and spiritual commons for the university, if not the city itself: a shared set of requirements for everyone, but also a symbol of the institution's link to national and global culture. As the Pathways mission statement puts it, this curriculum connects the "past to the complex world," and the present to a "fresh and enlightened future."[1]

This mission has its origins in the reading commons idea of the university. And it is a mission with staying power. That we can read our way into shared knowledge and culture is an idea that survived the Cold War, the culture wars, and the digital revolution, and it remains an important feature of the academy in the post-pandemic years. Even when they challenge its efficacy and use, scholars see a humanities core as a signature feature of the American academy; and the enactment of its reading

https://doi.org/10.7330/9781646425433.c001

commons idea of the university, a "radical democratic event" of history (Harpham 2017, ix).

This chapter revisits that take on American history, challenges its claim to democracy, and tells the story of an alternative idea of the university: an academic commons made in composition. From 1937–1940, Holland D. Roberts, a compositionist and labor activist, Walter V. Kaulfers, a scholar of foreign languages, and Grayson N. Kefauver, Dean of Education at Stanford University, recruited two hundred educators to teach and document ten thousand public school and college students enrolled in pilot language arts courses centered on writing. They got a grant to create a curriculum and called their experiment the Stanford Language Arts Investigation (SLAI). The SLAI investigators focused on institutions built to serve those new to high school and college: recent immigrants or children of immigrants, Black students, students who worked full- or part-time, and adults were the majority. Though the subjects they taught ranged from foreign languages to composition, the primary objective of the SLAI courses was the same: encourage informal student writing and count it as a resource, as "socially significant" cultural material (Kaulfers and Roberts 1937, 18).

Here we insert the SLAI into the history of general education as a brief but powerful disruption in the century-long reign of the reading commons. We explore the experiment's four monographs and classroom archives, describe its theory and practices, and detail the groundbreaking writing pedagogy of its researchers. I focus on the two primary leaders of the SLAI, Walter V. Kaulfers and Holland D. Roberts, and three educators affiliated with the project: literary scholar Louise Noyes, compositionist Alvina Treut Burrows, and librarian and curriculum reformer Charlemae Hill Rollins. Through classroom case studies, these scholar-teachers found that informal student writing created contact among diverse students, "rooted" students' cultures and literacies in course content, and "reconstructed" the university as a site for creating a "world society" of writers.[2]

That world society of writers was never actualized. By 1945 the SLAI was debunked, deemed dangerous, then lost to history. Returning to their experiment restores the Stanford Language Arts Investigation's study and practice of writing as a primary "binding experience" of learning and social life. "Binding experience" is the phrase a 1945 Harvard committee used to describe why the reading commons—literary canons and close-reading skills—should be the core of "cultural literacy." The SLAI's belief, that a knowledge commons could be built by students writing together in their public school classrooms, proved incompatible with this definition of cultural literacy promoted after World War II. We'll explore why the SLAI project failed to find a fit in the reform movement of the twentieth century, so that we can reclaim its vision for today.

INVENTING COMMON LEARNINGS IN EARLY AMERICA

Reading was written into the founding documents of the nation. Literacy scholar Deborah Brandt calls our attention to an early draft of the Bill of Rights, which included the "right to speak, to write, or to publish their sentiments." Draft copies do mention writing, but it was deleted from the final version, with no explanation. Brandt surmises that the founders decided to discard writing as a right—leaving freedom of the speech and press intact—because authorship was a "step too far" in the democratic project, a source of power too great for the ordinary citizen (2014, 4). Writing was for poets, playwrights, and professionals, not the masses.

Mass reading, on the other hand, was part of a spiritual and civic ideal; in political rhetoric and at the first colleges of the postcolonial period, reading was called upon as an activity that takes us into "shared belief systems" (Brandt 2014, 4). The academy's earliest mission statements depict reading as something to enhance the virtues of the public.[3] The terms "liberal education" or "liberal arts" were used to define courses that enacted common background knowledge needed to build community. The values of this community were passed down by writers of Ancient Greece and Rome, attributed to a humanist tradition of the West. Scholars in the classics created reading requirements to render "the common good" and provided what one nineteenth-century Yale report described as "discipline and the furniture of the mind."[4] Liberal arts colleges emphasized reading together, while research universities assumed private reading would provide discipline and furniture of the mind and the "social ethos" for a new nation (Dorn 2017, 10).[5]

Debate about which books created this ethos heated up in the late nineteenth century, as industry expanded and American schools looked to European models for expanding research.[6] Bowdoin College's A. S. Packard argued that an increasingly complex, diverse nation needed something stable and predictable to combat swift transformations in society. Packard rejected the more flexible curriculum being developed at places like Amherst College. He used the new term *general education* to highlight the importance of courses geared towards better living. Reading books in special ways and in certain classes offered a foundation for all human endeavors. For Packard, a generally educated person not only obtained broad knowledge, they also gained a methodology for living, a way to pay "attention" to ideas before becoming professionals (Wells 2012, 18–19).

In the latter part of the nineteenth century and the start of the twentieth, the classical, liberal arts curriculum got a public hearing and dramatic overhaul. Charles W. Eliot inaugurated his Harvard presidency by inventing an elective curriculum for general education and creating courses related to new industries.[7] Harvard's elective curriculum included writing courses but was defined by its synthesis of liberal arts, classics tradition, and the pursuit of scientific knowledge. A goal of Eliot's curriculum was to promote progress and make Harvard the institution to cultivate the nation's "intelligent public opinion" (G. Miller 1988, 15).[8]

Eliot's general education became a model for many colleges and universities. But some took exception to the claim that a nation's "intelligent public opinion" was crafted in a few courses and at just a few elite campuses. One challenge to this notion came from the architects of the first federally sponsored report on higher education, the 1913 United States Bureau of Education's *Economy of Time in Education*. This report included studies produced by many leaders of schools created for a growing student public. It was edited by the president of the recently built University of Colorado, James H. Baker. Baker, a contemporary of and frequent collaborator with Harvard's Eliot, also sought a modern approach to "common learnings."[9] That is the term he used in 1910 when he convened several committees to conduct a ten-year research study of the topic. Though not cited much as a general education innovator, Baker's report, and its research on public institutions, is an early example of an idea of the commons that went beyond reading the classics.

Much of this 102-page document published by the Department of the Interior centers on the conflict between vocational education and liberal education and between skills and specialized knowledge. Baker believed this conflict proved it was time for a "new definition" of culture courses (USBE 1913, 9). He suggested students connect big questions about "power" and "selfless" learning to practical activities of the classroom (53). An integrated approach to common learnings interested another member of this committee, Nicholas Murray Butler, president of Columbia University. Years later Butler became known as a top-down administrator whose support for World War I inspired fierce advocacy for a "War Issues" course, which eventually became part of Columbia's famous great books requirement. But in 1913, he was among the scholars making the case that the "college problem" can be solved through better "cooperation" between home and school or by creating "closer relations" between "knowing and doing" (57, 83).[10]

What might have happened if the academy had pursued general education as close relations between "knowing and doing"? This question motivated educators in marginalized schools. These institutions offered a range of suggestions for building a commons outside of the classics and liberal arts reading. Yet there is little scholarship about common learning experiments in these "new" twentieth-century institutions—normal schools, women's colleges, small liberal arts schools, Black colleges, and public state universities.[11] There are two reasons cited for this oversight. First, such experiments focused on small-scale, local, curricular studies and results were not published at all or only in reports rather than scholarly books. Second, these pilot projects often involved K–12 institutions as well as universities and colleges and have thus been disregarded by historians of the academy.[12]

I want to add a third reason for bypassing these alternative experiments in common learning. They redefined the humanities in the work of public school students and made the case that material created in classrooms contributes to a national and global culture. This is the "radical democratic" thinking that paved the way for the Stanford Language Arts Investigation and its interest in writing as an activity of the academic commons.

THE GENERAL EDUCATION MOVEMENT OF THE 1930s: TWO IDEAS OF THE UNIVERSITY

The Stanford Language Arts Investigation introduced their composition experiment at the start of the "general education movement" in the 1920s and 1930s. Historians describe the "gangly" state of the academy before this time, with no standards for admissions, graduation, or funding and almost no federal involvement in what was taught or learned (Thelin 2011, 153).[13] That didn't change until the first decades of the twentieth century, when enrollment increased by 50 percent (Snyder 1992). In the second decade of the 1900s, the junior college, an "indigenous American institution," became a significant part of the scene in the West and Midwest, enabling more students from rural and, eventually, urban schools to attend college.[14] Between 1890 and 1940 high school enrollments almost doubled every ten years and junior colleges grew, some connected to well-funded research universities and some independent and linked to vocational institutes.[15]

These transformations contributed to a national interest in higher education. But concern about commons learnings didn't become widespread until the start of World War I. In the 1920s, educators in the

United States took a "uniquely American" response to the global crisis by turning to education (Purves 1988, 3). "War Issues," the name of the first contemporary civilization course taught at Columbia University in 1917, expanded in the decade after and is cited by most historians as a first step in the pursuit of shared-learning higher education.[16] The Literature-Humanities requirement at Columbia followed in 1919, first as a General Honors course and then as a great books requirement for all. The core courses here influenced many other large elite schools, and soon "general education" became the preferred term for common learnings. By the 1930s, a "reform movement" took hold. Reformers were guided by two philosophies, liberal humanism and progressivism. These philosophies continue to inform the national conversation about common learnings and inform the curricula of major universities.[17]

John Dewey, the noted philosopher then at Columbia University, and Robert Maynard Hutchins, lawyer, writer, and young president of the University of Chicago, were leaders of the two approaches to the general education movement. Dewey believed in the elective or distribution model: skills and common experiences could lead to an engaged citizenry and an equitable democracy. Hutchins argued for a core system: common reading provides common background knowledge. In his famous *The Higher Learning in America*, Hutchins borrows from Columbia University's John Erskine to promote great books as a solution to what ails American culture. He believed that this curriculum was needed to stave off the "great evils" of civilization: communism, divorce, lawlessness, and most importantly, the "dilemma of isolation." America's problem with isolation and its lack of shared values, was, according to Hutchins, the crisis of the time. He blamed this crisis on progressivism and the confusion of "Americanism" (*The Higher Learning*, qtd. in Hofstadter and Smith 1961, 927).[18]

The term *Americanism* traces back to the eighteenth century, and the Americanization movement has deep ties to anti-immigration policies and to white supremacism.[19] But in the 1930s, progressive philosophers worked to reclaim this movement to support diversity and the sharing of power among classes and ethnicities.[20] Dewey's scholarship pushed against a "melting pot" view of Americanism and argued that a "genuine assimilation *to one another*—not to Anglo-Saxondom" is essential (Kazin and McCartin 2006, 93, emphasis in original). Drawing on research he conducted at the Laboratory Schools at the University of Chicago, Dewey saw common core courses as a source of unity. Education grounded in "contemporary science and contemporary social affairs" could do more to end "disorder" than reading the classics, he argued (Hofstadter and

Smith 1961, 953).[21] Dewey did not advocate for any one model; instead he emphasized courses that exposed students to the "study of social needs and social potentialities" ("President Hutchins' Proposal to Remake Higher Education" qtd. Hofstadter and Smith 1961, 951). This take on Americanism smacked Hutchins as rooted in an "erroneous notion of progress" (929). He thought of the university as a place to get beyond the present and towards the "permanent." And what was permanent was the "unity" gleaned from "the greatest books of the Western world" (938).

Despite Hutchins's criticism, Dewey's philosophy informed the direction of general education. Turning social needs and social potentialities into lesson plans for reading and writing led to a fertile period of experimentation in English studies.[22] Two examples of Dewey's work filtering into the language arts are in curricula associated with the life-adjustment and intercultural movements. The former focused on daily experiences of a child's personal circumstance, including health, well-being, and family life. "Intercultural education," an early version of multicultural curricula, engaged research in the social sciences and specifically in anthropology to forward the backgrounds and traditions of many cultures and encourage unity among youth (Burkholder 2008, 22–23). But it also served as a kind of accommodationist form of education, ignoring power dynamics and the history of violence and suppression of minoritized groups.[23] *English Journal* articles from the 1920s and 1930s focus on student plays, pageants, field trips, and literary readings representing a variety of cultures but not the historical or literary traditions of these groups.

The intercultural and life-adjustment movements changed the direction of composition teaching. Many scholars link the origin of writing studies as an academic field to general education courses and to the 1930s experiments of the National Council of Teachers of English (NCTE). These certainly influenced the "process" agenda of composition studies, with its focus on informal writing and student-centered teaching. The process movement is considered the first paradigm of the modern discipline of writing studies. Sharon Crowley's abolitionist argument—that freshman composition is politically bankrupt and does not belong in the academy—hinges on the potentials and ultimate failures of progressivism and the general education movement. She writes that composition courses went awry when they turned toward experience and humanism and away from rhetoric and "commonplace" concerns of culture. She traces how writing teachers joined forces with reformers of the 1930s and pushed for "unity" in communication (1998, 162–69). In the early 1970s, when process advocates distinguished composition studies from literary studies, they might have turned back to rhetoric and to

communal concerns. "Unfortunately," Crowley writes, process pedagogies over time reified liberal humanism and individualist progressivism.
And so the process paradigm lost its connection to social aims (165).

Also unfortunate is how little we know of the Stanford Language
Arts Investigation's unique, communal approach to writing education.
Crowley and other scholars are right to point out where experiments of
the progressive period led to individualist, "narrow goals" (Applebee
1974, 146). But they are wrong that the SLAI was one such project. The
few researchers who acknowledge the SLAI at all only focus on one of
its publications, *English for Social Living*, which was geared to teachers
connected with the NCTE and its sometimes "narrow" approach to
experience education. In turn, critics like Arthur Applebee fault the
program for not being concerned with "curriculum reformulation"
(150). Thomas P. Miller (2011), the only other writing scholar to address
the project, relies on Applebee's account. He concludes that the SLAI's
attention to practice "limited" the reach of the initiative, noting that it
was not "broadly engaged" in research (169).[24]

I think the limitation is our own. Historians, cultural critics, and
compositionists are quick to find intellectual and political engagement
in sanctioned scholarship and curricular reforms. The SLAI looked
elsewhere, to a third idea of the university, made in the everyday "scrap
parts" that collect when students and educators form knowledge despite
and in resistance to constraints (la paperson 2017, 52). In the 1930s, the
SLAI scraped material from knowledge and social collectives made in
the composition classroom. Their project offers a model for reforming
the intellectual commons of our own time.

THE STANFORD LANGUAGE ARTS INVESTIGATION,
1937–1945: A THIRD IDEA OF THE UNIVERSITY

Grayson N. Kefauver, Dean of the Stanford Education Department,
likely hired two new faculty members, Walter V. Kaulfers and Holland
D. Roberts, around 1935. Prior to coming to Stanford, Kaulfers and
Roberts invested in the reading commons idea of the university. Both
had experience with the progressive curricula promoted in schools and
at Columbia University in particular. And Roberts had been influenced
by humanist thinkers and especially by the literary critic I. A. Richards
and his "Basic English" curriculum, which aimed to stabilize the English
language to facilitate mass literacy and promote common learning.[25]

In addition to these influences, shared reading lists and small group
teaching were pedagogies important in the first stages of the SLAI. Early

experiments by Kaulfers and Roberts show the faith reformers placed in reading groups to forward common learnings. In a 1935 study of one thousand middle school students, Kaulfers and Roberts found that "community" goals, like "improvement of reading habits," "refinement in taste," or "promotion of international understanding and good will" could come from intercultural reading groups (Kaulfers and Roberts 1935, 737). Yet their research also acknowledged the failure of such pedagogies. They were disappointed to discover that the groups did not tap into alternative and fresh modes of making culture. This was a prescient critique of collaborative learning and would be echoed by writing theorists of our own time.

For the SLAI researchers, reading groups could engage students in texts but not in finding their place in an "age of informality" (Roberts and Fox 1937, 275). An informal age, as Roberts and Fox described it, is characterized by new kinds of communication and evolving ways of learning. In the public schools, students work, speak multiple languages, commute, and have experience moving between cultures. They need a place to make sense of transformations and problems in the contemporary world, in "unemployment, child labor, lynch law, vigilante violence, chauvinism, and war" (Roberts and Fox 1937, 282). While reading could help understand the world, it wasn't helping students participate in it. For that, Kaulfers and Roberts eventually turned their attention to writing.

In 1936, the two scholars drafted the grant proposal for the Stanford Language Arts Investigation. The first publications of the SLAI dutifully acknowledged the contributions of liberal humanism and progressivism. The SLAI leaders were seeking approval from the General Education Board (GEB), a funding organization deeply invested in both movements. The GEB would eventually support the SLAI, and as Kefauver had worked in national educational associations before, he was likely the connection to this foundation. Kefauver was certainly aligned with its mission to provide resources to new or underresourced public schools. But his conception of what a public school and university could do was limited. Kaulfers, like many GEB curriculum writers, championed skills courses for new students at institutions serving poor, immigrant, and Black students.[26] Core courses cultivating a cultural "intelligent opinion," as Harvard president Eliot once put it, were for other kinds of schools and students.

The first monograph of the Stanford Language Arts Investigation, *A Cultural Basis for the Language Arts*, breaks from this view and illustrates the different direction Kaulfers and Roberts wanted to take for their pilot project. Kefauver's name doesn't appear on this publication, and while it does in other monographs, he is never cited as an author of any of the SLAI essays. That is likely because by 1937, Kaulfers and Roberts had developed an alternative program for public education, the language arts, and shared knowledge that deviated from the skills-based curriculum favored by many General Education Board grants.[27] They coined their proposal an experiment in "creative and constructive Americanism."

Americanism was an important term for the general education movement, as we explored earlier on in the chapter. In part, Kaulfers and Roberts were motivated to join the movement in order to reclaim Americanism as a project for education justice.[28] The two define this term as an effort to end the "chauvinistically suppressive" content and pedagogy undergirding general education programs that overlook the "potential resources" and "rich cultural background" of "new" students attending "new" schools (Kaulfers, Kefauver, and Roberts 1942, 16; Bulletin 35).

By "new student" the SLAI leaders mean "Negro" students and "native American" students, who inhabited the land before Europeans brought their systems (Kaulfers, Kefauver, and Roberts 1942, 273). They also mean anyone concerned with the cultures and literacies happening in junior colleges, adult extension programs, interdisciplinary public high schools, colleges, and workplace literacy programs. At a time when there were few such institutions, Kaulfers and Roberts wrote that the public school student and teacher should not "receive" standards and "culture" "through the back door" like a "scullion-maid before entering the parlor" (Kaulfers and Roberts 1937, 47).[29]

It's important to stress how radical this was.[30] The SLAI was not interested in a public college version of Columbia or Chicago's great books program. Instead they proposed a three-year study of writing in "new" high schools and colleges. These were mostly in the West, though there were participating schools in the Midwest and Texas. Educators in the SLAI could teach any course they want related to the humanities or social sciences or foreign languages. Classroom teachers would also be researchers, gathering every summer to learn pedagogies that promote integrated writing practices and scholarly approaches that stressed "contact" composition "rooted" in the cultures and literacies of students (1937, 4).

Two theoretical essays, published in multiple versions throughout the monographs, outline these foundational beliefs. In "Rooting the Language Arts in American Life and Culture," Kaulfers situates student writing as a resource of culture and finds this resource in the "orientation" classroom or any "*from the beginning*" language arts course (1942,

7, emphasis in original). This essay draws parallels between the work of student genres and the work of farmers or city planners, the "builders" of institutions and ideas. The analogy between composition practices and urban and agricultural development makes for some purple prose and broad claims that "immigrant" communities are the "new frontier" of democracy. Kaulfers acknowledges systemic racism, ignorance of Indigenous cultures, and anti-immigration policy in education. But he insists that classrooms are spaces to realize the power of the new public (1942, 279). Kaulfers draws on Roberts's 1937 NCTE Presidential Address to define power:

> From half a lifetime of teaching writing to people of all ages from Kindergarten through the sixties I know that every person has potential power to write. Anyone who says a true word of his own has created . . . Why then, is the writing of books, songs, plays, and poems so unusual a thing? We have only to study the natural child at play to find speech growing out like mountain flowers . . . We must help children to find something interesting and worthwhile to say and build an audience situation that will give them reasons for saying it. The form of their production is to be thought of only in judging the effectiveness of *what* is said to *whom.* (Kaulfers 1942, 281)

The power of student writing is the way it reveals the public's expression of self and other, and can "prevent us from reverting" to "masters" (1942, 268). We scholars are susceptible to masters; we've been trained to locate knowledge in accepted forms. Kaulfers suggested that informal discourse can redirect attention and epistemological energies. He argued that one way to avoid becoming masters of ideology or curriculum is to read and create "collective" pictures of student writing. Another way to avoid mastery was to remake the idea of the university. The SLAI's new idea of the university is explored in another long essay, "A Reconstructive Language-Arts Curriculum in Action." This piece has no authors as Kaulfers and Roberts offer it as a "composite" study, built on the work of two hundred SLAI teacher-researchers and thousands of students. The essay reads like a memoir or travel narrative, with a "tour guide" and "visitors" who walk through the writing and reading "laboratories" of a language-arts course. At one point in the tour, the guide stops to show visitors the "manila folder" stuffed with informal student writing, cards, and letters. She describes how writing accumulates in the laboratory and becomes a source for a "list" that evolves and expands in dozens of filing cases. The classroom visitors are full of questions about those file cabinets. Most of these questions—about whether the SLAI writing exhibits poor grammar, about whether casual discourse is allowed to be used in academic papers, about challenges that students new to the English language face—will be familiar to contemporary composition teachers or administrators. The teacher replies that "mistakes" happen and are explained in context, that academic writing changes just as public writing changes, and that informal compositions done often and in multiple languages improves engagement. But what matters to this teacher is that we pose other kinds of questions about student work. The SLAI asked a version of one question, over and over again. How can composition become a "vital concern" of the academy, so that it can "reconstruct" the society? (1942, 244, 239).

That question guided my reading of this archive and my research into the archive of the twenty-first century classroom. But before we explore these file cabinets of culture, we need to acknowledge the limitations of the Stanford Language Arts Investigation, as it worked then and as it serves as a model for today.

First, the leaders had their blind-spots, especially regarding race. While Kaulfers and Roberts made the case that a commons could be made in practices of students left out of white supremacist, anti-immigrant public and educational policies, they don't acknowledge their own position. Along with Kefauver, they are two white, male professors leading a public school and college experiment where the students and sometimes teachers would often be working class or poor, the first in their families to go to college, of color, speakers of languages other than English, recent immigrants, or children of immigrants. Some of the educators involved in the SLAI were part of the labor movement and early Civil Rights efforts. Others trafficked in jingoistic claims of the intercultural movement and progressive initiatives popular in the 1930s. Teachers talk of "tolerance," "peace," and "broader understanding of racial groups" as they seek "world friendship" so that their courses could avoid "possibility of war in the next generation" (1942, 216, 220). I try to point out where the project lapses into naivety, ignorance, or biased assumptions. I also work to highlight those areas where the teacher-researchers struggled with their own biases and took a risk we educators often fail to do: ground a large idea of the university in the low-stakes writing activities of everyday students.

Second, the archives and monographs are incomplete and not always categorized by course or level. The archive reveals a dizzying array of themes emphasized in the pilot courses. A few of the classes resemble today's digital humanities courses, as they focus on analyzing, critiquing, and participating in new media environments. Students often generated public projects like community radio programs for their campus or neighborhood community. Other courses were text based. For example, one class traced the linguistic origins of all the names of the towns in Arizona. Another, "How to Survey School Lighting," was labeled a "humanities" requirement because its focus was "critique" of "everyday life." In this course students collaborated with a Stanford professor at the Illumination Laboratory, union workers at a lighting factory, and each other. They map out their school and home lighting and electricity systems. Some of the maps were crude and simple, hand-drawn and clipped to traditional five-paragraph essays. Several were more complex and detailed, involving models and mathematical equations (Bulletin 47; Bulletin 46; Bulletin 19; Bulletin 59).

The SLAI participants did not share one pedagogical view, syllabus, assessment measurement, or research protocol. We know little about the backgrounds of the particular teachers, we don't have access to their research notes, and there is no record of an assessment measure. Yet there were some consistent practices: every teacher in all subjects prompted students to write in informal genres repetitively, and much of this material was collected and studied over three years and then, with student permission, made into course content and published for additional classrooms, teacher education, or scholarly publication.

Understanding the diversity of material but recognizing this singular focus on writing helped me make some strategic decisions about what to include in this history. Of the four monographs and eighty archived bulletins, the informal writing practices that appear most frequently are (1) a form of freewriting, or spontaneous, in-class, timed composing and (2) reflective letter writing, or written correspondences between students and among teachers, students, and members of the public. Three educators affiliated with the SLAI were especially forthright in exploring the democratic and radical uses of these forms. Louise Noyes, world literatures teacher and community organizer, was interested in "contact composition" as a kind of writing that creates course content; Alvina Treut Burrows, compositionist and reading scholar, thought "free writing" a form of institutional knowledge and another kind of cultural content; and Charlemae Hill Rollins, NCTE researcher and editor of the first anthology of Black writers taught in K–12 schools, used reflective letter writings to rethink reform in education. Their research and pedagogy articulated a vision that deserves to be read today.

CONTACT COMPOSITION: CONTENT IN
THE ACADEMIC COMMONS

"Composition" moves the environment of the classroom, of the institution. That was the theory behind Louise Noyes's SLAI world literatures course. "Builders Together" was her case study of that course, which focused on spontaneous timed writing activities and the relationship between such writing and the surrounding environment. She and the SLAI leaders believed that such work contributed to fostering "points of contact" between self and other and between classroom and culture (1937, 4). When students write alone together over periods of time, they break routine and document knowledge as it moves into the present, and this "roots" their cultures and literacies in history. If these student artifacts were integrated into course content, Noyes thought they could help "development" of institutions so that they account for the knowledge of a changing public (1942, 216).

Noyes's idea about contact and content defied the dominant position of the day. A few years before Noyes started teaching, Abraham Flexner, in his widely read 1930 polemic, *Universities*, equated "contact" with a polluted educational model. Flexner was a national leader of reform; in 1910, his Carnegie survey of medical education prompted an overhaul of specialized, professional training. Later, as a member of the General Education Board, Flexner moved from surveying programs to denouncing them.[31] Flexner analyzed several common learning experiments and found them lacking. Many programs promoted "contact" with the world rather than "intellectual content" (qtd. In Hofstadter and Smith 1961, 916). Contact "extended the reach" of knowledge out of traditional disciplines and into schools with "new" types of students. Additionally, Flexner found that contact courses engaged with problems, "practice," and, worst of all, writing (Universities qtd. Hofstadter and Smith 1961, 916). Though many of these classes were taught at "lesser" colleges, even a few "great" institutions like Columbia University offered "critical writing" and "persuasive speaking." For Fletcher, these offerings only insulted the American public (Hofstadter and Smith 1961, 916).

Not for the first or last time in history, composition is put in an impossible position. Writing is simultaneously everywhere and invisible, the essence and insult of American life. Fred Newton Scott, rhetorician and contemporary of Flexner, used his leadership roles as Modern Language Association and NCTE president to describe this "paradoxical" predicament of composition (Scott 1913). For Scott, paradox, or knowing and doing, to use the phrase of early common learning experimenters, was essential for democracy, radical participation, and shared knowing. And for Louise Noyes of the NCTE, this paradox was essential to intellectual vibrancy.

In "Builders Together" we learn how to put this paradox into course content. Noyes's case study opens by asserting the importance of building a culture of the classroom through literacy activities. This work was different from other "culture building" classes, like those taught in intercultural or great books core programs. Noyes admires many of these initiatives, especially the Dewey-inspired "experience"-focused NCTE curricula. But she believed that the progressive teaching of culture was too "conservative" (1942, 216). In repetitive, collective composition, cultures and literacies are not merely acknowledged or experienced but are part of a project to expand authorship. She considers informal student writing "productive" because it can engender an "idea" of the student's "own community" and how that community gets written rather than mastered (1942, 216, 219). When practiced often and in the company of others, contact composition, like "free writing," produces genres that neither conform to a particular idea of the past nor predict a future. These genres are artifacts of culture itself, they are made to be "moving" in the present (1942, 216).

Noyes taught in high schools and two-year schools in Santa Barbara, California. Here, she found that students and often educators travel back and forth between environments and cultures, among "publics." She argued that education needs to travel too. Noyes believed that freewriting was a discourse that emerged at the meeting point between an individual and their community, between one student's past and the present conditions of the classroom and surrounding "atmosphere" (215). I think of this discourse as knowledge made in the middle. Middle-made knowledge assumes students come in with background knowledge that is a resource for learning and culture. Noyes encouraged students and educators to build new social and intellectual forms with their backgrounds by freewriting frequently and ritually. After doing so, Noyes tracked patterns of connection, detailing where student work deviated from prescribed course material, and she entered these deviations in her summary of course material.

As an example of this content made in the middle, Noyes described a project where students write as they visit neighborhood monuments and after reading literature related to these monuments. These freewrites are, like all of the SLAI student writing, collected over time. In some cases, they'd become material for a group-written report or final essay. Sections of this work are written in Spanish and translated into English by the students.[32] In another project, students create a twenty-page syllabus with over a hundred texts they recommend. Also included in the syllabus are two policy reports, a dozen articles from local magazines and newspapers, demographic studies of the city produced by students and professors at another college, and annotated literary maps of Santa Barbara. These include "relations" between their "environment" and the cultures of Latin America. Many other student-authored projects are on that syllabus, including the essay "Analysis of Women Leaders in Mother-Owned Shops in the Mexican-American Community." That essay is part of the reading list used in another section of a world literatures course, taught a year after Noyes's experiment. What we see in the archives are student freewrites found as key texts, just as the *Anthology of World Poetry* and the *Anthology of World Prose* were. These literary anthologies were edited by Mark Van Doren and Carl Van Doren. The Van Doren brothers were Pulitzer Prize winners (Mark for poetry, Carl for a biography of Benjamin Franklin). And Mark Van Doren was an architect of Columbia's famous common core curriculum. In SLAI syllabi and lesson plans, such titles sit alongside student work.

Usually a reading list comes to us in neat linear progression, a rundown of required or canonical works. Here, such lists are interrupted by statements from students. For example, a junior college professor collected a semester of student freewrites and published them, without editing, as part of the reading curriculum for future SLAI teachers (Roberts, Kaulfers, and Kefauver 1943, 69). One student's text explained that freewriting often and as part of an encounter with canonical texts allowed her to place learning in the local and larger context of her life. "Days are like people," the student remarks, something she realizes from her own writing and from reading student work alongside published material (Roberts, Kaulfers, and Kefauver 1943, 108). For the SLAI researchers and students, writing that happens "in connection with" the reading curriculum becomes the curriculum (Kaulfers, Kefauver, and Roberts 1942, 247).

Interjecting writing that is "in connection with" meant that content was contingent on emergent thinking. Further, reading lists formed in the "in between" meant that canons were not transcendent but tied to local cultures and literacies. That makes these lesson plans nonlinear, often very long, and sometimes hard to follow. And we can't know how much of which texts listed in the archives were actually read. But this course material makes a point about learning: it happens in moments not always captured by official, sanctioned curricula. In these classrooms, informal, spontaneous freewriting was a social action, a genre that broke with the Eurocentric canon and asserted student desire as content-making material.

This is not how freewriting is taught or studied today. Though cited often as a classroom pedagogy, freewriting does not usually get discussed as cultural or intellectual material. However, the compositionist Ken Macrorie, thought of as a modern pioneer of freewriting, looks back to the 1930s to offer a different origin story and purpose for this practice (1991, 173). He cites two books as sources for freewriting's beginnings in the academy, Dorothea Brande's popular self-help manifesto *Becoming a Writer*, published in 1934, and the little-known volume *They All Want to Write* by Alvina Treut Burrows, Doris C. Jackson, and Dorothy O. Saunders, published in 1939. Brande's book is mentioned in composition scholarship, but Burrows and *They All Want to Write* are not.[33]

They All Want to Write is a study of student writing. But it's also an event in this history of the composition commons. Alvina Treut Burrows began her career in the early part of the twentieth century as an elementary school teacher, became a New York University professor, then an educator in reservation colleges and an activist for the Students' Right to Their Own Language movement, and finally, a historian of composition studies (Cullinan and Hopkins 1996). Her interest in classroom research prompted her engagement with the progressive-era experiments sponsored by the NCTE, which brought her into a relationship with the SLAI.

In the mid-1930s, Burrows applied for funding to conduct a small-scale study of writing activities happening in the growing elementary school population. Burrows, Jackson, and Saunders began the study documented in *They All Want to Write* with one hundred students in Bronxville, New York, and Montgomery County, Maryland. A grant supported these teacher-scholars as they conducted autoethnographic studies of classrooms in order to observe and identify "dimensions of expression" (Burrows, Jackson, and Saunders 1939, 2). The research focused on studying two "types of communications," practical and personal. Burrows presented these as the most common forms of discourse produced in classrooms. Personal writing takes place in diaries, letters, and notes passed between and among persons, and this is not material that belongs to institutions or commercial endeavors (2). "Practical" genres are informational, like the five-paragraph essay about an assigned topic or a letter to the editor of a newspaper responding to a published article about local politics.

Burrows and her team produced case studies of dozens of public school classrooms. They eventually extended their research to hundreds of students of all ages and areas. Once they collected the artifacts of personal and practical genres, they noticed, just as the SLAI educators did, that there were "many forms" of "abundant" knowledge that surfaced in the personal writing category. These were not all private nor relevant solely to that individual (Burrows, Jackson, and Saunders 1939, 84). One of these forms was "free writing." We don't know where Burrows learned about freewriting, but we can assume that her time with the SLAI was influential, as she adopts the same language for the practice as Noyes does in her contact composition case study. In describing one common pattern in a diverse set of artifacts, Burrows observes an "environment" or "atmosphere" that emerges from these artifacts. The atmosphere is created in three ways: the texts call up a student's past experience in writing, conjure another student writing in the moment of writing, and make a connection between the background knowledge and the present act of composing. She described this as the genre's ability to "effect power" for the classroom, the institution, and the public (Burrows, Jackson, and Saunders 1939, 5).

Atmosphere and power can be "elusive" (Burrows, Jackson, and Saunders 1939, 174). Throughout the book, Burrows and her colleagues are sometimes vague about how freewriting can engender change. The freewrites reveal "spontaneity" and "surprising gains in language power" (5, 61). Burrows and her colleagues also find freewrites proof that "a sense of mutuality" forms in composition (172). None of this could be pinned down or proven. Still these researchers insist that this kind of writing is essential for democracy because it can create authors, enlisting "considerable attention" of readers (172).

Burrows asks scholars and educators to enlist their attention, too. We might respond to this request by noting the differences between these SLAI-related writing projects and the reading-centered idea of the university. The purpose of studying great books or acquiring skills and experience in general education curricula was to ground the present in a shared past and progressive future. In *They All Want to Write*, the purpose of contact composition is to notice how attention forms and moves between self and other, and in relation with the local institution and a larger culture.

The kinds of contact compositions depicted in these classrooms vary, as do the ways teachers and students pay attention to them. For example, one group freewrites while moving through a museum on a field trip and then shares their work with others. Another group freewrites while sitting on the rug of their library and chooses whether or not to hand these in to the teacher or keep them. Burrows and her colleagues described one elementary school classroom that made freewrites into public art. Other classrooms kept the artifacts private, available only to the researchers. A few classrooms used poetry and literary forms as models for what we might now call "directed prompts" while other classrooms asked students to engage in mini ethnographic projects, recording student conversation about texts and then freewriting based on those scripts. However, throughout her study, Burrows, Jackson, and Saunders marked how often the freewrites acknowledged a particular feeling and experience students have while writing with others. These freewritings were concretized contact with student histories. They revealed how individual pasts connected with where they may go next as writers and thinkers. The particular pedagogical exercise did not matter much to Burrows and her research team. Instead, the ritual of repeated, frequent, and codified writing opportunities mattered, so that the immediate knowledge-making of classrooms was understood "constructively" (Burrows, Jackson, and Saunders 1939, 84).

Freewriting is constructive when, in the act of composing, it builds a shared vocabulary about writing. Burrows, Jackson, and Saunders created a list of categories that define that shared vocabulary. This included desire, experience, personality, observation, media, and tension. They were "reality" made in "difference" with emergent "encounters" of communication, and Burrows believed, like Noyes, that they add to "institutional knowledge" (1939, 11, 9, 84). Institutional knowledge can come from demographic statistics, policy reports, and analysis of material conditions. And institutional knowledge can come from the content of contact composition.

Later in her career, Burrows extends her thinking on composition and institutional culture. In a 1950 essay titled "Caste System or Democracy in Teaching Reading," she underscores a growing movement to categorize and assess students into competency. The focus of her essay is on reading instruction and group work, what we now call "collaborative learning." She found that reading groups and collaborative writing activities, gaining popularity in the 1940s and 1950s, were becoming another form of standardization that denied the cultures and literacies of students and contributed to a "caste system." Today, group work is either considered a source of true social bonding and shared learning or proof that schools erase conflict and cultivate conformity (Bruffee 1984; Duffy 2021; Holdstein and Bleich 2002; Trimbur 1989). Burrows takes the position that group work is a form of curricular monitoring (Burrows 1950, 145). Freewriting and other kinds of informal compositions are certainly susceptible for surveillance too. But Burrows and her team hoped to find ways to avoid this, to keep this genre out of the hands of those who "rank" and reform curriculum (145).

In her history of the nascent field of composition studies, Burrows considered again how to avoid a "caste system" in education. Writing in 1977, Burrows's essay "Composition: Prospect and Retrospect" praises the rise of the process movement and its focus on reflexive and extensive writing (Burrows 1977, 41). But it also asserts the need for more case studies of writing, more scholarly research on classroom cultures, and more accounting of student work as it emerges in the social setting that is school. Such studies might, she believed, promote new authors of society and avoid institutional conformity (1977, 31). If we are looking for a "radical democratic event" of history, then Louise Noyes and Alvina Treut Burrows's plan—that composition counteract an educational caste system and make contact with emerging cultures—seems a good place to start.

LIVED-IN LETTERS: RECONSTRUCTING THE ACADEMIC COMMONS

Like Alvina Burrows, SLAI leader Holland D. Roberts had researched writing and collaborative learning and was especially concerned with reading and its role in a changing educational climate.[34] Roberts's early scholarship on book clubs concentrated on the potential for groups to help with comprehension and meaning-making. He was especially interested in what the SLAI educators called the "X-ray technique" developed by literary critic I. A. Richards. The X-ray technique was another term for "close reading." Recognizing the pedagogical possibilities of this approach, it makes sense that Roberts and Kaulfers enlisted Richards as a consultant for the SLAI. We find Richards named as "counsel" in the SLAI's published monographs (1942, vi), and his work is cited throughout the archives (Bulletin 35). The SLAI believed close reading was important for individual growth and common learnings. Especially important for Roberts was the way close reading can cultivate a shared "attitude toward language." Roberts took that phrase from Richards's *Basic Rules of Reason* and *Practical Criticism*. Both books were essential to scholars of the day and SLAI participants.[35]

Practical Criticism is known to most literary critics. Whether we read the book or not, the typical English major will recognize its subject, close reading, as an essential activity of the humanities. The most cited story of that book is the account of Richards's classroom case study. In one of his literature courses, Richards took identifying marks off of published poems, students interpreted them, and then their responses were coded as evidence of readerly assumptions, potentials for error, and the challenges of paying attention in a complex, mass-culture age. That anecdote of teaching has become a linchpin in histories of theories of reading. And it has marked Richards as a pioneer of New Criticism, an approach to reading texts widely adopted at all levels of education.

A canonical text for historians of literary criticism, *Practical Criticism* should also be understood as critical to the formation of the American academic commons. Along with serving as a consultant to the SLAI from 1937 to 1945, Richards was involved in multiple general education reforms. Like many liberal humanists, Richards saw reading as a way to manage the powerful transformations of the mid-twentieth century. In 1944, the last year the SLAI published material, Richards became a member of the Harvard committee charged with creating a vision for general education that could be adopted for the postwar student public. Before and after that, Richards pursued the cause of social "unity" in higher education (Richards 1929, 287).

In one of his treatises on general education, Richards referred to the "world crisis" of minds corrupted by technology and war, "*more exposed than ever before*" (1947, 232). The humanities could alleviate this crisis and offer "defense" against "generations of dehumanized animals" (Richards 1947, 236). Richards called for teaching "reverence and regard for famous books" and "direct" attention to these texts (Richards 1947, 234). One way to direct attention to culture and tradition is to practice reflection alongside close reading. Roberts believed that reflection helps with the "imaginative understanding of things in common" and that this understanding brings together "the work and the reader." Bringing reader and text together could make students enlightened, deliberative, and possessing of a more "conscious" "attitude toward language." That attitude was needed for mastery and for a civilized culture (Richards 1929, 315, 319; Graff 2008, 177).

At first, Holland D. Roberts and the SLAI team embraced Richards's strategies. Then they confronted their limitations and resisted, wrestling with Richards's understanding of reflection and cultural education. Roberts's earlier studies of reading groups led to his concern about the way close reading might narrow what and how students would read. He conjured the theoretical essays written with Kaulfers and thought that reflection should happen in writing genres and be part of a "reconstructive" approach to texts. Reconstructive reading, Roberts argued, assumed that building culture of any kind required interaction with emergent thinkers, writers, and texts. Writing would be essential to this kind of reading. Roberts believed that students and teachers would encounter published texts and write back to them, reflecting on their relationship with this content, and then offer this writing as additional and alternative course material. This kind of correspondence could happen in letter writing or genres that support a "live-in" connection (1937, 5). I have adopted Roberts's discussion of reflective writing and called this form "lived-in" letters.

Like freewriting, reflective cover letters have a long history in the field of composition and in the scholarship on liberal education. Kathleen Blake Yancey (2016) describes multiple generations of scholarship focused on reflective letters (5–6). However we don't often hear about letters as genres that can "reconstruct" our reading and idea of the university. For Roberts, one way student letters reconstruct the university is by being another way to get "close" to reading. For example, in a course about semantics and composition, students spent each period exchanging index cards. Students used one side of the card to reflect on a reading list and the other to write about several texts they discovered on their own. In this activity, students read for "commuting," or to move their thinking into connection with diverse authors and views of the world. After a semester of creating such cards, students would be responsible for writing lived-in letters to libraries and educators (Bulletin 35). In one example of a lived-in letter, an undergraduate writes to another about a course's reading list and its inclusion of Steinbeck's *Grapes of Wrath*. He talks about that novel, but also of his "observation and evaluation" of the novel's place in the class and in the larger experiment of the Stanford Language Arts Investigation. The student sets out to compose another letter, not just to "Wilbur" but also to "the President," about the place of this book next to other course curricula (Roberts, Kaulfers, and Kefauver 1943, 152–53).

Roberts turned to reading material curated by one colleague in particular, Charlemae Hill Rollins, to explore the power of lived-in letters. Not often associated with composition-rhetoric, Rollins is instead known as the first Black president of the American Library Association and creator of a groundbreaking anthology of Black writers. The anthology is the result of Rollins's influence in the National Council of Teachers of English (NCTE) and her time as a librarian at the Hall Branch of Chicago Public Library from 1932 to 1963. During these years, Rollins set out to diversify the content and the patrons of the library. She expanded acquisitions and created spaces for writers, both famous and little-known, including Langston Hughes, Gwendolyn Brooks, Zora Neale Hurston, and teachers in the local public schools (Turner 1999). While doing this work, she was commissioned by the NCTE to create a new bibliography to aid educators and librarians in choosing Black-authored books for their institutions and curricula. That became the anthology *We Build Together: A Reader's Guide to Negro Life and Literature for Elementary and High School.* A monograph-long list of fiction, history, and biographical texts, this pioneering collection centered on African American characters and communities. Compiled first as a pamphlet in 1941, *We Build Together* was used in schools and colleges in the decades immediately following World War II (Applebee, Langer, and Nachowitz 2010, 178). Literacy scholars name this collection as central to the NCTE's efforts to broaden reading lists in English departments and consider the collection to be an early example of culturally responsible course content and a precursor to later-century diversity and inclusion reforms (Miller 2003, 201–3). One scholar connects *We Build Together* to anti-racist pedagogies and the rise of critical race theory (Mabbott 2017). In addition to these contributions, Rollins's legacy matters as an advocate of a composition commons idea of the university.

Rollins was not directly involved in the national conversation about general education. Yet she proposed an alternative approach to reading and to course content for the language arts. She was influenced by the progressive experiments initiated through the NCTE and the liberal humanistic projects of general education reformers. However, Rollins also pushed back on intercultural curricula. She believed that social justice could happen neither by expanding core courses or canonical readings nor by celebrating multicultural traditions.[36] A "fully integrated" democracy required "fully participating" in the ongoing evolution of this anthology (Rollins and Edman 1967, xi).

Roberts also sought a broad, action-oriented interpretation of diversity and thought. In the SLAI archives, we see how classrooms engaged with the stories of Black life in *We Build Together* as reading material. More telling, we see evidence of students paying special attention to one feature of the collection: the "list" of criteria used by Rollins to determine which writers belonged in the anthology. Rollins's list of necessary criteria for entrance fell into three categories, "illustrations, language, and theme," and she collected names and short descriptions of books that belonged in genres ranging from picture books and fiction to folklore and poetry. That list became a writing prompt for students in the SLAI. In Roberts's classrooms, students create their own "writing list" to pair with Rollins's reading list. They did this reconstructive work with their "lived-in" reflective correspondences.[37] The goal of this activity was to expand representation of Black authors but also allow students to reflect on the list, communicate to others about it, and become authors of "life as it is now" (Rollins 1967, 4). These student-generated lists were often shared with the authors and editors of course texts, like Rollins, and was a source for expansion of this anthology, to include additional categories, from science and sports to fiction, history, and biography (Rollins 1967, 4).

Reflective writing played an important role in the making of Rollins's anthology and in the way teachers and students engaged with it for their SLAI courses. When graduate students, educators, or librarians consulted with Rollins about curricular revision or text acquisitions, she often referred to student reflections. She quoted from students' letters to make the case for a particular author's inclusion or to suggest ways to make these lists more respond to student perspectives. In workshops and classrooms, Rollins asked students whether a book had pictures of Black persons that were defined by "discrimination" (Rollins 1967, xii). Another item on the criteria list was "dialect." Her work with students distinguished dialect from linguistic or literary interpretations that are "overdrawn" and "chiefly derogatory" (xii). Rollins wanted *We Build Together* to come alive, to be "read and lived, rather than looked at," and that required frequent revisions to her list of Black writers (9). Reflective letter writing enabled the SLAI teachers to "consciously and systematically" make classrooms contributions to "social purposes" that are integrated in to "everyday life" (Roberts, Kaulfers, and Kefauver 1943, 318, 318). Rollins and her colleague Marion Edman acknowledge the influence of letters in the final edition of *We Build Together*. Their introduction to the 1967 printing describes revisions to the anthology and how it changed in response to feedback from educators and students, the "action" needed for real educational justice (1967, x).

Lived-in letters were essential to Roberts's understanding of diversity and democracy. Rollins believed that reflective notes enabled society to understand "developments in history" and the "struggles for human dignity" (Rollins 1967, xii). A simple list of reading enumerates content, it offers a linear, uniformed set of texts. But what the SLAI called a "list of writing," as invented in these courses and in lived-in letters, represents the aggregate belongings of this group. Curricular reform here is built with a collection of background knowledges that roots shared knowledge and common experience in student writing.

In the decades that followed the SLAI, Rollins's anthology evolved in editions published from 1941 through the last publication of 1967. Each volume was a product of its time but also a process of responding to the letters of students. In a foreword to the anthology written in 1963, one educator hoped that this evolving curriculum may become a "best seller" (Crosby 1967, iii).[38] That never happened. Indeed, we know little of Rollins's efforts nor of Roberts's lived-in approach to them. Only a few years after Roberts brought *We Build Together* to the Stanford Language Arts Investigation, this radical experiment linking composition with reading lists was forgotten. And so was the SLAI's history-making idea of diversifying curricula in reconstructive practices.

CONCLUSION: TAKING RESPONSIBILITY

In the final years of the SLAI, Kaulfers and Roberts convened symposia, published research, and hoped to get more scholars interested in the project. They recognized that their findings offered no "specific formula . . . or any particular type of curriculum organization" and no "unifying" theory. And their experiment often produced data hard to categorize. The SLAI leaders seemed to believe it would be adapted anyway. Perhaps their enthusiasm masked nativity and blind faith in institutions that would support a project focused on minoritized, public students. Kaulfers and Roberts knew their work needed "solidarity" because the "day-by-day" documentation of emergent, diverse cultures and literacies was a large undertaking—a big, radical, democratic endeavor (1942, 394).

The SLAI did not attract many partners or much solidarity. Some critics found the program unwieldy and hard to replicate. Others called it a threat to a unified Western world. In an *English Journal* symposium about the SLAI, Robert C. Pooley (1944), University of Wisconsin professor and director of its Integrated Liberal Studies program, faulted its lack of pedagogical consistency (236). Charles Pendleton, a self-described "moderate progressive," declares the SLAI a manifesto of "radical pronouncements" catering to the "have-not" "in culture or worldly goods" (1944, 125–26). As the war came to an end, early supporters moved on and the SLAI researchers went separate ways. Kaulfers got involved in international education while Roberts, who continued to teach writing and contribute to the labor movement, was forced out of his faculty post at Stanford because he refused to sign a loyalty oath. The rest of his life was spent with the California Labor School (Durst 2017, 233). After 1946, we hear little about the publications or experiments of the SLAI.

While most scholars and teachers turned their backs on SLAI, one mid-century educational reformer urged scholars to take another look. The feminist compositionist Lou LaBrant described the SLAI experiment as a challenge to teach writing as critical to dissecting "big social" issues and to consider how doing so might make composition a focus of education. She believed the academy could be a space to do this work.

LaBrant posed a set of questions we might ask ourselves again, in the present. Can the academy carve out one place where the primary focus is on "intelligent communication" that serves something larger than curricular goals? Can this intelligent community be in service to new forms of knowledge made by the public? Can it help create a commons made by students: a "world society" of writers (LaBrant 1944, 125)?[39]

These were not questions the academy of the 1940s was ready to answer. As we will see in the next chapter, the postwar reformers had other plans for an idea of the university and for engendering a world society. But for the SLAI, paying attention to the cultures and literacies of public school students was not just an idea, it was a way to practice a "democratic way of life." That way of life demanded more than completing a close reading of certain texts. Charlemae Hill Rollins insisted that it demanded authorship and depended on readers who took on "responsibilities" (1967, xi).

In restoring this writing-centered history of the academic commons, we answer Rollins's call to be responsible readers. That work continues in the next chapter, as we track the legacy of this history over the twentieth century and into today. Doing so enables us to be "builders" of a world society of writers as it forms in the classrooms and academy of now.

2

FROM CULTURAL LITERACY TO COMPOSITION, 1945–PRESENT

Education should be a source for dynamic engagement with "the needs of the children of democracy." Research and teaching must honor that knowledge happens in the embrace of stability and uncertainty. And culture materializes in emergent, contact and reconstructive writing. These were the core principles of the Stanford Language Arts Investigation (Kaulfers and Roberts 1937, 1). The SLAI leaders understood that such ideas would not be easy to enact. In times of great change, it's natural to want the security of "paradigms" or to seek refuge in a "unifying factor" of life. The allure of "drill masters" is that they seem to settle us when we don't know what the future will hold (Kaulfers, Kefauver, and Roberts 1942, 268). And no one in 1945 had a firm grasp on what the future would hold. The SLAI followed on the heels of the depression, piloted courses during World War II, and documented findings on the precipice of unprecedented technological and cultural shifts that would come with the Cold War, the labor movement, the Civil Rights Movement, and women's rights.

The academy today also faces great transformation. And we too seek salvation in curricular unity and disciplinary paradigms. Educator and activist Tania D. Mitchell calls the second decade of the 2000s a period of "multiple pandemics." Mitchell uses this term to describe the particular crisis resulting from the Covid-19 outbreak and the aftermath of the racial justice protests of 2020 and 2021, which followed murders of Black people by police. These crises were part of problems that preceded the pandemic but exploded after decades of defunding public higher education, inequity in admissions, and the mounting costs of college.[1] Before 2020, we believed in some kind of shared vision for the university.[2] Afterwards, we desperately need it.

How we enact this vision depends on where we believe a commons can be formed and what it can do. Some humanists have seen the academy as a place to outpace the future, creating disciplinary specializations that can predict skills and innovate for new networks of knowledge. And

https://doi.org/10.7330/9781646425433.c002

some have seen the academy as a place to put down roots, to find solace from the present by seeking timeless truths that provide a shared path but also a "unifying" purpose for society.

The SLAI chose neither. These educators, many of them K–12 teachers, did not belong to college English departments, were not pioneers of any one discipline, and while advocates of new media and access to technology in classrooms, were not affiliated with communication or composition studies. They resisted the allure of a national curriculum and recoiled at the notion that required reading made social connection. They looked at great books courses and core curricula sprouting in schools and colleges and saw loss: the loss of a "public" and its "power to write" (Kaulfers and Roberts 1942, 281). A new age required new ways of educating; the SLAI realized this. But they thought disciplinary specialization and the pursuit of a shared heritage in reading lists was not the direction to take. Instead they fought to have students write alone together, to promote expansive forms of authorship and a world society of writers.

This chapter asks what happened to that view and how we can restore it. First we explore the last years of the SLAI and the development of the general education movement in the Cold War period. How the reading commons, and its primary theory of knowledge, cultural literacy, came to dominate the idea of the university is intimately tied to the death of the Stanford Language Arts Investigation. Then, we track how cultural literacy influenced the culture wars of the last century and directed the competency reforms of this century, recording how this approach failed to bring a diverse student body into the work of building a shared public. At the end of the chapter, we reframe contact composition and lived-in reconstructive practices of the 1930s as critical for the academy of today.

CULTURAL LITERACY IN THE COLD WAR

Much has been written about the "golden age" of the academy.[3] The unprecedented growth of higher education that took place between 1945 and 1975 and the changes in American culture that came with them are topics of debate and considerable discussion across disciplines and in the public.[4] The goal in this section is to consider an underexplored feature of this period: the rise of the reading commons idea of the university. Cultural literacy, or shared knowledge generated by common reading, propelled this rise.

The student population explosion, technological innovation, and the pursuit of geopolitical influence brought increased attention to higher education's role in a changing world order. The GI Bill is the most famous federal policy of this period, aimed initially at educating veterans, later paying the tuition for half of the males attending college, though largely benefiting white males (Smith and Bender 2008). Vannevar Bush's 1945 treatise, *Science: The Endless Frontier*, followed up on this policy, bringing federal dollars to STEM research and the humanities. President Truman's Commission on Higher Education added more money and clout behind a new proposal for America: that higher education was a "national resource" for a new era (Menand 2010, 40).

The Truman commission called the mid-twentieth century a time of "reeducation" (Smith and Bender 2008, 85). Many policymakers believed that the next generation of Americans, distraught by war, was devoid of connection. A shared curriculum could provide a singular purpose for a diversifying student public.[5] Scholars cited the "plethora of crises" following the war; they turned to common core courses and humanities-centered reading lists a kind of "safety valve" for the nation, with cultural literacy the epistemology to provide that safety. Soon, general education went from a movement to a "matter of social policy" (G. Miller 1988, 141, 110).

The story of how cultural literacy became a matter for social policy takes us back to the Stanford Language Arts Investigation. Journalist and French professor James B. Tharp was an early champion of the SLAI's "worldmindedness" (1939, 301). But in his last review of the SLAI, he determined that the postwar world needed unity of purpose and curriculum. The "worldmindedness" of the SLAI and the proclaimed "power" of practice were deemed experiments of another day. Essential for a new era was a centralized vision. Tharp defines this new vision as "cultural literacy" or "language study as common learnings among thinking American citizens" (Tharp 1946, 23).

This was the first time "cultural literacy" appeared in print. It wouldn't be the last. We next see the term in the 1945 Harvard publication, *General Education in a Free Society: Report of the Harvard Committee*. Spearheaded by Truman Commission member and Harvard president James Bryant Conant, this manifesto, committee report, and argument for making common learnings a national agenda defined cultural literacy as we think of it today: common background knowledge.

In most histories of the American academy, *General Education in a Free Society* is named the founding document of general education, influencing most of our nation's programs.[6] Conant's introduction to the Red Book, called this because of its crimson cover, situates the report as ushering in the new reform period of the 1950s. General education links the two approaches to common learnings that dominated the 1930s:

the liberal-humanist and progressive approach (1945, vi). This Cold War compromise combines the work of Hutchins and his great books program with the progressivism of Dewey and his social skills agenda to create cultural literacy.

The Harvard committee named "heritage" texts, literary studies, and close reading the material, subject matter, and methodology for generating national unity in the post-war years (Harvard Committee 1945, 77). Exposure to great literary works and "close study of well-written paragraphs and poems" had a "formative and ordering power" on the mind (112, 110). Conant identified this power as exactly what was needed to provide "sufficient educational background for citizens of a free nation" (Conant 1945, viii). Background knowledge is the "cultural literacy" necessary to gain "continuity with the past" and to give the "binding experience" that holds democracy together for the future (135, 102).

The report had its share of critics, especially at Harvard, where many of the curricular suggestions were rejected. But its influence was felt beyond this Ivy League institution.[7] I. A. Richards, literary critic and one-time Stanford Language Arts Investigation consultant, is considered the "essential" member of the Harvard committee. He was responsible for elevating literary studies as the "central humanistic discipline" of general education (Harpham 2011, 136). Like President Conant, Richards had been concerned about a "cultural crisis" in America. And like Cardinal Newman, whose idea of university sought to transcend time and place, Richards believed that close reading of heritage texts could save society from itself, even as it crafted a new educated public (1947, 236).

Richards's ideas about crisis and literary studies had a profound effect on American culture. How reading might combat chaos and foster tradition became a topic for the popular as well as scholarly presses. We can see how cultural literacy became part of the national discourse in looking at one noted collection of essays, the 1954 *Is the Common Man Too Common?* Edited by National Book Award–winner and one-time compositionist Joseph Wood Krutch, this collection presents the post-war "boom" in higher education as a problem for America. Krutch was suspicious of cultural literacy especially, because he believed widespread reading would not yield critical thinking. Shared reading and cultural literacy for the masses was not enough to combat "world crises." What a changing and growing population required was depth and critique, or "uncommon excellence" from outside the "common" educational system (1954, 19). This sounds elitist, but Krutch believed his position radical, a way to combat conformity. Reading, when done by the right people and in the right places, was the only rescue from the "tyranny of the average" and the threat of corporate culture, with its mass production, middling media, and "mechanization" (Krutch 1954, 18).

I. A. Richards believed that close reading of heritage texts created civilization. Krutch believed that too much reading could corrupt culture. Either way, reading was a weapon in the Cold War battles about national identity and education. In the next decade, this fight moved into arenas outside of the university and literary journals. In the 1970s, cultural literacy became a compelling curricular mission for K–12 schools, especially teacher preparation programs. In 1973, for example, the Department of Education at the University of Arizona devoted resources to a new Cultural Literacy Laboratory. The architect of this program was Herbert B. Wilson, who had been involved in Stanford University's International Development Education Center and various mid-century reform movements. After World War II, several international education programs were created at large universities. Some prepared teachers for cultural literacy programs overseas. Others, like the Cultural Literacy Laboratory, focused on domestic concerns, promoting intervention in the nation's "helping professions" (1973, 4).

In his 1973 report, Wilson explains that the term *cultural literacy* was coined in an essay about "instruments" for teaching effectively in the elementary school classroom (1973, 2). Though wrong about the source of the term, the error is telling. It shows how cultural literacy became associated not only with heritage books but also with the social sciences and "instruments" of "interaction skills" (Wilson 1973, 3). These skills are described as "communicative" and "intercultural" and are measured in questionnaires about students' attitudes to religion, ethnicity, race, class, and sexuality. Stressed here is the teacher's ability to understand common responses to culturally sensitive questions and to use this understanding to help students "transfer" their thinking from one circumstance to another (7). Knowledge transfer, a critical learning outcome for today's composition classrooms, was defined here as necessary for "multicultural classes" and "target populations" (1). The "target populations" included "bilingual" students, the "American Indian," and the "culturally diverse" of "rural" or "urban" areas (2). Future teachers assessed "readiness" to encounter the other, engaged in "impact tasks," and diagnosed their "culture shock" (2).

Years later, critical pedagogues challenged this version of cultural literacy and argued for a place-based, practice-oriented approach to pedagogy and curricula (Bowers 1974).[8] But the promise of a unified society proved too strong a pull, especially at the end of the century, when education was called on to solve other kinds of cultural and literacy crises.

CULTURAL LITERACY AS CONTENT IN THE CULTURE WARS

In his 1992 book *Culture Wars: The Struggle to Define America,* sociologist James Davison Hunter looked at the post–Vietnam War era, the conflicts between identity groups that flourished afterwards, and a "crisis" in American character. He considered the outsized role schooling, and especially the syllabi of humanities courses, plays in the making of the nation's self-image. Hunter defines schooling as a means of "reproducing community and national identity" and the curriculum of the university as especially important for guiding the "next generation" (Hunter 1992, 198, 211). Culture wars are, in part, clashes of generations. And a generation's big ideas are learned in books taught in school. When we expand, challenge, and critique books, the nation notices. It's natural that literary canons and cultural literacy lists become ground zero for America's culture wars, explains Andrew Hartman in his twenty-first-century update to Hunter's study. What we read is who we are. For Hartman, a list of books is a representation of Americanism, a platform for us to ask, "How should Americans think?" (2016, 223).

Americanism was a critical issue in the general education movement. In the late 1980s, this concern surfaced again. Books about the state of the American mind became reading material for students, scholars, and politicians.[9] One of these books was E. D. Hirsch's 1987 *Cultural Literacy: What Every American Needs to Know.* After a decade of scholarship on literary and composition theory, Hirsch published this surprise bestseller about education.[10] His research determined that Americans were thinking less than they had in the Cold War. Hirsch blamed progressive education for the problem and called for a return to teaching shared content and common reading lists. Hirsch's take on cultural literacy incorporates some of the instrumentalism of Wilson's teaching laboratory with the liberal humanism of I. A. Richards. Like his predecessors, Hirsch believed that teaching humanistic background knowledge was part of a strong domestic and international geopolitical agenda. A shared core would enable equity across class, race, and geographic boundaries; lead to better standardized test scores; and improve America's standing on the world stage.[11]

Soon after Hirsch's book came out, "cultural literacy" became a commonplace term for policymakers. It was debated on national television by presidential candidates like conservative Pat Buchanan, and triggered campus protests and curricular reforms at institutions like Stanford and the University of Texas at Austin.[12] But while credited with creating the term, Hirsch merely offered a remake of the Cold War idea that reading is the tie that binds. And he made a more ecumenical case for cultural literacy as content. He avoided talk of value and great books and defined background knowledge as originating in both literary texts and in the "network of information that all competent readers possess" (Hirsch 1987, 2).

Hirsch's "network" for competent readers came in the form of a list of what everyone "needs to know." He argued that this cultural literacy list did not celebrate one culture over any other and believed public schools need not "take political stands" or get involved in syllabus battles (Hirsch 1987, 137). Yet his reading list became a kind of canon, spurring curricular reforms throughout the nation. In the late 1980s and 1990s, politicians aligned with the Reagan-era "back-to-basics movement" relied on Hirsch's book to limit the reach of ethnic, Black, and gender studies. That's because without dissecting how cultural literacy lists get made, the default standard became the list Hirsch said mattered. This may not have been Hirsch's intention, but it was its outcome. Cultural literacy became synonymous with certain content and universities praised or blamed for delivering this content.

The notion that the university was a business disseminating the content of culture was exactly the concern of Joseph Wood Krutch. His Cold War critique of cultural literacy was grounded in a fear of commodification by state and corporate values. Krutch wanted a higher purpose for knowledge and thought universities should pursue "uncommon excellence." However, as the twentieth century was coming to a close, many believed that both uncommon excellence and cultural literacy were myths. In 1996, Bill Readings described higher education as corrupted by conformity. "Excellence," Readings explained, had become one with consumerism and the production of "optimal input/output of information" (1996, 39). The "university is in ruins," declared Readings, titling his famous book with a variation of this phrase. No longer the guardian of national culture—what Kant called the "university of reason"—the academy of the 1990s had become an instrument of transnational capitalism.

The University in Ruins opens with the claim that what we used to call "liberal education" is extinct. The university can no longer be meaningful to the public good, because there was no public, no "common reader" to devour or ignore lists of great books, or any other kind of curricula. The university has lost its "referent." In turn, Readings thought the academy needed to find another idea to believe in for the new century (50). His idea for remaking the university is to see it not as a tool for the nation-state or for civilization creation but as a place where "*the question of being-together is raised*" (20, italics in original).

That's a good suggestion. Indeed it had already been made, in the 1930s classrooms of the SLAI. And it is one that continues to be asked in composition courses, if we bother to look there. Readings, and the cultural studies and critical university studies scholars who followed up on *The University in Ruins*, could have considered contact composition and lived-in reconstructive practices as places to pursue being together. But instead educators and policymakers continued to conjure content from the past and teach certain skills they predicted would be needed for the future. And the idea of a composition commons remained dormant.

CULTURAL LITERACY AS COMPETENCIES IN THE TWENTY-FIRST CENTURY

Even as the canon wars died down, cultural literacy remained a quiet presence in the national conversation. In the first years of the twenty-first century, a different kind of reading commons energy occupies the academy and public. After the financial crisis of 2008, and in response to calls for reforms brought on by globalization, digital transformations, and decades-long demands to address racial, class, and gender inequities, "cultural literacy" as a mission resurfaced. This time cultural literacy was not about timeless canons but urgent competencies needed for the unknown to come.

One polemic that helped launch the new era was the 2011 *Academically Adrift: Limited Learning on College Campuses*. Written by two sociologists, Richard Arum and Josipa Roska, *Academically Adrift* argued that the uniquely "complex" culture of the twenty-first century made teaching and learning especially challenging. However, their explanation of today's digital, distracted culture sounds strikingly similar to the description offered by the Harvard committee writing at the end of World War II. Both declared students as living in a time of "crisis." And the solution to the crisis was, once again, "general" skills accumulated from close reading of important books.

Arum and Roska name a host of problems with the academy of the twenty-first century. But "limited learning" is most pressing. Their study of 23,222 students from two dozen four-year institutions found that undergraduates did little sustained academic work and that their thinking, writing, and learning skills were not improved from their four or more years of college (2011, 35–36). They used the CLA, the Collegiate Learning Assessment, as their measurement tool. The CLA is a standardized test that assesses growth in "general skills," specifically critical thinking, analytical reasoning, problem-solving, and written communication competencies. Their analysis concluded that there is "widespread agree-ment" that these skills are the "foundation for effective democratic citi-zenship and economic productivity." And students were sorely lacking these capacities, especially in sustained reading and the ability to write about reading (Arum and Roska 2011, 11). While these skills could be taught in any course, it was in general education and introductory writ-ing classes where they were emphasized.

Fewer higher-ed polemics of the last decade were as influential as *Academically Adrift*, noted the *Chronicle of Higher Education*.[13] Countless "soul-searching" books about the university and especially about read-ing followed. And so did dozens of curricular changes, assessment poli-cies, and general education updates.[14] For example, the Common Core State Standards (CCSS), directed at K–12 schools, was a national reform that came out of reports on general skills and their new importance for learning. The English Language Arts Standards of the CCSS, used in forty-two states, outline "direct assessment" rubrics to measure critical thinking, writing, and reading capacities. One of the critical capacities for college and career readiness sounds like a skills-oriented version of Harvard's 1945 theory of close reading. Students need to "read closely to determine what the text says explicitly and to make logical inferences from it." They also need to "cite specific textual evidence when writing or speaking to support conclusions."[15]

Since 2012, colleges have joined K–12 schools in adopting competency measurements for learning, like the Written Communication Value Rubric. Created by the American Association of Colleges and Universi-ties (AAC&U), this rubric seeks evidence that can be shared nationally to show that students are prepared for "complex challenges." The AAC&U defines close reading as the "examination" of knowledge and as essential "preparation" for the twenty-first century.[16] One Pew report discussed President Obama's turn to common core competencies as a way to compete in a global economy. The "future of higher education," this report declares, is nationwide attention to the "competencies" of a complex society. One such competency is the ability to manage the information overload, and another is to practice "close reading."[17]

What counts as "core" courses shifts. Yet close reading of important texts is as central now as it was a century ago.[18] In composition and general education courses throughout the country, close reading and deep learning are two of the most common outcomes.[19] CUNY's general education program, "Pathways," took on much of the language from the AAC&U and CCSS reforms, even for courses that no longer follow these rubrics. At Lehman College for example, we've revamped all of our required liberal arts and English department offerings. But we maintain a commitment to this cultural literacy skill of close reading. Whether the course is on Shakespeare or composition or Latinx literatures, students must show mastery in close reading of central texts.

In the 1940s, close reading of the Western canon provided cultural literacy that could cultivate a "great civilization." In the 2000s, close reading yielded cultural literacy that certifies basic competency needed to survive the new century. Reading to survive is the thesis of Nicholas Carr's famous 2011 essay "Is Google Making Us Stupid?" That essay was expanded upon in his Pulitzer-Prize-finalist book, *The Shallows*, reissued in 2020. Carr argues that most of us are drowning in the sea of conflicting, chaotic information. In the time of Google, "deep reading" has given way to shallow searching. The result is a society confused and alone. Without the "concentration" and "contemplation" of close reading, we are stressed out, stratified, and sad. Carr argues for a return to the rigor that comes with direct, private encounters with books. He does not name specific books, except for Plato's *Phaedrus*. What he does offer is a warning that the full depth of the human experience is at stake if we stop reading deeply.[20]

In this version of cultural literacy, reading rescues humanity, saving us from the distractions of the present. But more recently, reading is an agent of change for humanity, the stimulant we need to make a better future. If we have an educated, well-read polis, we will have a better American commons, Eric Liu (2015) argues. Liu, Carr's colleague at *The Atlantic*, wants to harness new media for advancing an old democratic ideal: learning and equality for all. In his 2015 essay "What Every American Needs to Know," Liu moves away from "depth" and cites breadth of knowledge as central to an increasingly divided and diversifying America. In 2015, the culture wars were "raging along quite nicely," Liu wrote. And with them, "Americanness and whiteness" were finally becoming "delinked." It's time, Liu argues, for the nation to earn a "new way" to be American. Ironically, this updated Americanness sent him back to an older idea of the commons, and to E. D. Hirsch. In the late 1980s, Hirsch created a cultural literacy list to make a "shared cultural core" for the nation. Liu wrote that this shared core was important once again, at the dawn of a new century.

Though he acknowledges the limitations of Hirsch's list, namely that it was made by only a few academics, Liu proposes a return to "background knowledge" as "right" for "common culture." In the information age, Liu suggested that background knowledge could be crowdsourced by "everyone" and then read, revised, and remade by that crowd. Like a handful of pundits and professors of the time, Liu put his faith in digital platforms and in the humanities as two vehicles for remaking meritocracy. Kevin Carey, in his book *The End of College*, and Thomas Friedman in the *New York Times*, were two loud voices championing this digital "revolution" in higher education. This should be the era for the "university of everywhere," with the most esteemed scholars from the most prestigious schools providing "abundant" and "free" education for all (Carey 2016). Carey and Friedman declared this in the early 2000s. But by the start of 2020, it was clear that MOOCs—massive open online courses—and other technologies could not fix education or bring equity to learning.[21] Since 2015, when Liu opined about the internet as an equalizer and Carey announced the end of college as we knew it, social media has enhanced divisions and prohibited cross-community interaction. We've had lower graduation rates in distance learning courses, with data showing low-income students perform worse in online courses than in face-to-face classes.[22] By 2019, Carey concluded that distance-learning programs were "schemes." Echoing Krutch and then Readings, Carey calls on universities to hunker down and rediscover their "fundamental" nature.[23]

What was fundamental for the SLAI educators of the 1930s were students and the cultural material that comes from shared learning. But this was not a formula policymakers or critics of the twenty-first century followed. Whether meditative and melancholy, polemical, or data-driven, our influential critics continue to advance a reading commons idea of the university. For example, Columbia University professor Andrew Delbanco's 2012 *College: What It Was, Is, and Should Be* presents the university, and especially humanistic study, as a source of "the democratic promise," where everyone can "immerse" in the "joy" of learning. The "rich, middling, and poor" should all have the opportunity to "embrace the chance to think and reflect before life engulfs them" (Delbanco 2012, 35). Delbanco advocates for this opportunity and advances the humanities in his role at the Teagle Foundation. Cited widely since its publication, *College* began an important discussion about higher education and the growing inequities of our time. This work brings needed attention to initiatives that support historically marginalized institutions, like CUNY, hit hard by the pandemic.[24] However, Delbanco's vision of college, as where we go before "life engulfs," limits the nation's idea of what an academic commons can do, where it can form, and how it can be made.

In public, commuter composition classrooms like my own, the engulfment of life never gets dropped off at the campus gates. And being "adrift" leads to some powerful writing and thinking. No doubt

Delbanco and other champions of humanistic inquiry believe this can be true. Yet many of the most listened-to thinkers hold onto an idea of the university that depends on reading as sanctuary from lived realities. Christopher Newfield, an important advocate for public education, has pointed out the hypocrisy of politicians who defund the liberal arts and also demand better critical thinking and engaged citizenship. Yet to make his case, he reaches back to the reading commons tradition. In his 2016 *The Great Mistake*, Newfield details a "decline cycle" in public higher education. One way out of this cycle is to insist on the mission to "deliver mastery learning and creative learning" by drawing on the "venerable humanistic definition of the uses of the university" (Newfield 2016, 323, 328). That tradition is traced back to cultural literacy and to Harvard's *General Education in a Free Society* (Newfield 2016, 330). A few years later, in a pandemic essay, Newfield astutely points out how the "gig academy"—the reliance on underpaid and overworked adjunct faculty—is one way the "decline cycle" has worsened.[25] Yet he again returns to the reading commons for relief. Newfield refers to the 2011 polemic *Academically Adrift* to marshal evidence that our institutions don't support "deep learning." Calling up *Academically Adrift*'s claim that deep learning comes from a focus on close reading reifies the notion that innovation and "creative capacities" are invented by the humanists at prestigious places, to be handed down to the public academy. Indeed that is what Newfield argues: "Creativity learning . . . must be extended from the elite colleges and universities to public regional and community colleges" (Newfield 2016, 333). Extending this kind of learning honors the "venerable humanistic tradition" (Newfield 2016, 328).

The limits of this tradition are clear. It draws lessons on creativity and community and on learning and shared knowledge from one source: reading at elite universities. Might it be time to try out another tradition? And while we're at it, might we also venerate new content for a different kind of academic commons?

These are questions the reading commons can't address. Its idea of the university was never intended to notice, let alone venerate, the intellectual camaraderie made by students whose commoning happens despite, and sometimes because of, the adriftness and engulfing of life. If we are to engage the cultures and literacies of this public, and if we believe in the making of shared knowledge in the university, then we need to cultivate spaces where the academics commons is being written anew.

In 1937, when the SLAI centered their experiment in classrooms with public, nontraditional students, there were not many examples of such spaces. Today, they are where most of us teach and learn. And in those classrooms, the SLAI found that informal writing was a vital source for generating shared knowledge. This was an unorthodox view in the 1930s, when much of the discourse about culture centered on reading and when venues for writing and publishing were few. Today, we have multiple platforms for authorship. It's time to find social connections in these places and practices.

COMPOSITION AND THE COMMONS IN
THE CONTEMPORARY ACADEMY

Writing is an activity that occupies the lives of today's students and the public. Composing done outside of school for work, pleasure, entertainment, and community connection—"life writing"—is more commonplace and popular than ever before. Writing is ubiquitous, as Andrea Lunsford and her team of researchers at Stanford show.[26]

Technology is the obvious reason for the explosion of writing. Yet digital technologies, proliferating and powerful as they are, are not the only reason why we are communicating differently in the twenty-first century. The nature of work has changed, centering writing and the "making and managing information and knowledge in increasingly globalized settings" (Brandt 2014, 3). Writing forms publics and "counterpublics," or social entities that rise up alongside and in opposition to dominant constructs of power and privilege (Warner 2002). How we live is bound up with how we write; the lines between home and work and between private and civic life have blurred. As many rhetors have argued, humans are part of an ever-complex "ecological" network of communication; we are agents that are always surrounded by systems, entangled in them and participating in recreating structures of identity, power, and being (Inoue 2015, 78).

We know that more people are writing more than ever. And we know that writing is a dynamic, evolving, diverse activity. This reality is described by literacy researcher James Paul Gee. Gee talks about literacies that "nest" within each other. He distinguishes between primary and "lifeworld" discourse and how integrating the two is part of being a member of and participating in a communication-evolving society. We continue to create social languages, to "experience and language boot-strap each other" (Gee 2014, 80). Gee sees our complex literacy environment as requiring someone or something to say things like "pay attention to this here" so that we have ways of "looking at and cutting up the world" (81).

The SLAI teacher-researchers believed that informal writing looks at and cuts up the world. It pays attention to the ways we make contact with the shifts in time. And it creates the condition for collective experience and knowledge. That is a belief I encountered in practice, through my research in Lehman's composition courses. And it is a belief shared by many in the field of composition-rhetoric. Writing studies, as the field is commonly called today, has a role to play in constructing a contemporary academic commons. We can turn to certain traditions in this discipline to realize the rhetorical and social power of practice.[27]

When the SLAI began its experiment, writing studies did not exist as we know it now. The growth in student population, the birth of general education, and the increased funding for research in communication during the Cold War period ignited interest in composition as a field distinct from English (Goggin 1999). The inaugural meeting of the Conference on College Composition and Communication, the first national organization for the teaching of writing, occurred in 1949, just as the general education movement gained momentum. Many of the first essays published in the journal *College Composition and Communication* centered on first-year writing courses and their role in progressive and liberal humanist agendas for common learnings. In 1961, the relationship between writing and general education continued, when the National Council of Teachers of English got an influx of funds from the National Defense Education Act to develop Project English. That conference brought scholars together to consider "integrated English programs" that connected linguistics, literary studies, and composition.[28]

The Dartmouth Conference of 1966 followed up on Project English. Historians trace the origins of the modern field of writing studies to this meeting of American and British educators. Moreover, the Dartmouth Conference helped inaugurate the process movement in composition, critical to the growth of the discipline. Some critics characterize this movement as a form of "neo-progressivism" initiated by British scholars like James Britton (Miller 2011, 190). Britton and others urged their American counterparts to rethink their singular focus on literary studies and to tend to issues of cognition, expression, and practice.[29]

Though "process" was declared a paradigm for the field in 1982, the writing process movement emerged at the tail end of the "boom" age of higher education and in the wake of a growing, diverse, nonwhite, student population (Villanueva 2003).[30] The process paradigm moved attention away from the polished, finished text to the habits, contexts, and conditions that shape a writer, a writing task, and how we teach writing (Perl 1995).[31] Many American scholars associated with this movement, like Janet Emig, Linda Flower, John R. Hayes, Sondra Perl, Nancy Sommers, Peter Elbow, and Donald Murray, studied the cognitive features of writers. But many distanced themselves from expressivism, highlighting instead the social, collaborative features of writing-to-learn pedagogies.[32]

Two of these pedagogies were freewriting and letter writing. Both were central to the SLAI classrooms, referred to by this experiment as contact composition and lived-in, reconstructive letters. However, today we think of these practices as products of the 1970s process paradigm in writing studies. Freewriting, nonstop writing, is one of the first steps students use in the "general procedures" of the writing process (Lauer 2004, 129 [quote]; Tobin 2011). Likewise, reflective letter writing is considered an outgrowth of the first phase of the process movement. Reflection was promoted by researchers influenced by the liberal humanism of I. A. Richards, as we've seen, and by educators and philosophers like Lev Vygotsky, Michael Polanyi, and John Dewey. In the 1970s, reflective writing was important to writing courses, as a final step in the composing process (Yancey 2016, 1).

In the late 1980s and 1990s, during the social turn in writing studies and at the height of the culture wars, process pedagogies were scrutinized for their political naivety. Freewriting was often defined as a spontaneous practice meant to "remove almost all normal constraints" in writing (Belanoff, Elbow, and Fontaine 1991, ii). But instructions for how to freewrite often include very specific restrictions, prompting practitioners to write in one space, without stopping, for a specific amount of time. Writing scholars point out the contradictions of a practice that purports to liberate yet imposes rules. Lisa Delpit (2006) sees racial blindness in many process pedagogies, with their assumptions about liberatory ideologies, steeped in white, middle-class experiences. Hannah Rule focuses on problems with the freewriting prompt, which assumes that all learners can infer how to engage in open-ended assignments (2013). Anis Bawarshi notes how heuristics like freewriting traffic in "fantasy" because they assume one can write in a stateless, wandering, no-where's-land (2003, 176, 17).

Similarly, reflective cover letters aim to teach students self-assessment and mastery of their own thinking. These letters ask students to recount their composing practice and thus encourage metacognitive skills and self-knowledge (Yancey 2016, 5–6). However, scholars have questioned whether these narratives are authentic examples of reflection or, rather, places where students can perform a self, reproduce dominant ideologies of progress, and assert the "right" interpretations (Jung 2011).[33] Letters and freewrites, indeed all process-oriented pedagogies, can assume that individuals have some control over the confines constructed by society. But as David Bartholomae argued, to write is to face conflict and complexity, because we are never "free from institutional pressures" or "from the influence of culture" (1995, 64).

Writing-process pedagogies are still prevalent in composition classrooms and research. But they rarely are the subject of disciplinary disputes. Today, many educators think of these pedagogies as neutral tools devoid of serious controversy. Freewriting is said to promote interest in course content and to help with invention (Elbow 2012; Hinkle and Hinkle 1990). Reflective writing encourages "rhetorical sensitivity" and metacommunication, necessary for knowledge transfer (Shipka 2011, 117; Taczak and Robertson 2016, 43). And process-oriented pedagogies are among the many practices that form the "threshold concepts" in the field of writing studies. Threshold concepts provide a way to understand paradigms—a disciplinary past—and secure a path to a professional future: what's "critical for epistemological participation" (Adler-Kassner and Wardle 2015, back cover).

Threshold concepts matter for naming the contributions of writing studies to the academy. But we also need the academy to honor writing for its role in making a commons. For the SLAI educators, freewriting and letters could do more than enact epistemology or enable paradigm shifts. Freewriting and letters were not free from institutional or social constraints. Indeed, these classroom activities embraced tensions and, in turn, became forms of liberatory connection.

CASE STUDIES OF THE COMPOSITION COMMONS

In the next half of the book, we bring this historical study up to date, looking at case studies of the commons enacted in contemporary composition classrooms. In chapters 3 and 4, we examine an archive of over two hundred writing samples from forty-five students enrolled in two sections of English 111 at Lehman College. I track links between findings from these artifacts and the work of the Stanford Language Arts Investigation. However, my study does not match up to the SLAI in scale. Given the number and diversity of US institutions, I did not believe I could, or should, create a research project in service of a nationwide policy. Instead, my findings come from a small sample. The limitations of my research are the limitations of any case-study taking place in certain conditions, and I work to address them. These classrooms cannot be representative of all composition courses or practices. Still, I believe that the artifacts studied here offer direction for reorienting the academy to an idea of the university as a composition commons.

All of the artifacts collected in my research emerged from a classroom context, where particular pedagogies and curricular guidelines prompted them. Throughout the study, I read these artifacts with my various identities, one of them as a scholar and teacher of composition at the same school in which the writing classes are offered. I address the disciplinary, institutional, and intellectual contexts undergirding the production and reception of these texts. However, my focus is on how the artifacts prompt shared knowledge and a new idea of the university, and my attention is on the "world society"–making properties of this writing. For this focus, I draw on scholarship focused less on threshold disciplinary concepts and more on social practices of authorship. Taken together, we see how doing informal kinds of writing *in* the academy, with student authors *of* the public academy, does something *to* the academy.

This idea is steeped in the history we've just encountered: a tradition that names contact composition and lived-in reconstructive writing practices content for creating a commons. And it is based on three principles. First, my study is focused on the cultures and literacies of the new academic majority: nontraditional students who attend public, nonselective colleges. Second, it is suited to the literacies of our day, recognizing the dominant role that writing plays in creating shared knowledge. Third, it draws on scholarship from the field of composition and rhetoric, especially from genre studies and the pedagogies and practices developed by multimodal, anti-racist literacy pedagogues. These principles guide my research, but they do not belong to one discipline, ideology, curriculum, pedagogy, or institution. Instead, they contribute to a twenty-first-century idea of the university as a composition commons.

3

WRITING FOR CONTACT

"Write for fifteen minutes about anything or what you want. You may keep it, turn it in with your name on it, or submit anonymously."

This prompt, projected on the screen and printed on the front of a sheet of paper placed on the desks, welcomed us as we filed into Carman Hall, room 311, on September 5, 2012. It was the first day of my participant-research project in English 111, but the second week of class. I had missed the first two sessions. Lehman's fall term begins the week before Labor Day, when most schools and day care centers are closed for summer break. I had written to the professor a few days earlier explaining my child-care conflict. She wrote back that I was one of many students who needed to arrive late and catch up: "Just come in when you can."

On week two I came in, along with nine other students who had started their first semester of English 111 late. That day, the class of twenty-five of us responded to the freewrite prompt you see above. And we did so six other times over the course of fourteen weeks. By the end of that semester and after one more term taking English 111, I'd have an archive of one hundred and seventeen samples of fifteen-minute responses to an assignment given exactly the same way, with the same language. Our responses varied greatly, and so did our mediums. Some composed on laptops, others on paper, and a few of us in notebooks or phones. Sharing the freewrites was optional. We could pass it to our professor, but did not have to; if we did, she would take our names off and type up excerpts to share in class, which would eventually be put on our class website.

I no longer have access to that website, as it was erased weeks after my research project concluded. But I do have a phrase that brings me back to that classroom. It appeared on the handout and was coined by Xavier, the first student to speak aloud.

"So about this list of writing," Xavier asked, flipping the handout back and forth in his hand. "Do we continue with the material here or begin afresh?"

https://doi.org/10.7330/9781646425433.c003

I have already introduced Xavier at the start of the book. And we'll learn more about him later on in the chapter, as I got to know him in the course of my classroom research. But at this point, he was the student sitting in the front row with a name tag that read "manager" stuck to an oversized blue jacket, which he wore despite the heat. On that first day of class, I wrote down his phrase "list of writing." I didn't understand why. I couldn't yet know that "list of writing" would be a term used throughout the samples I'd collect over a course of a year. Nor could I know it was a phrase I'd find again and again while spending time in the overly air-conditioned library at Stanford University, where artifacts from a 1930s general education experiment were archived. *List* was the word Charlemae Hill Rollins and Holland D. Roberts used to describe what students do to contribute to a required curriculum. They found that when students write their own lists they change what counts as cultural material and remake society.

Xavier's list of writing helps us link the world society from the last century to the one forming in this century. And it begins the effort of reclaiming composition as central to commons-making.

We have spent the last chapters tracing the history of cultural literacy as a theory supporting a reading commons idea of the university. Here we turn the page on that story, focus on the contemporary academy, and observe how student writing contributes to new intellectual collective. The freewriting artifacts discussed here initiate this observation, starting with Xavier and two other student writers, Kammie and Ashley. From their freewrites, we move to the larger sample composed in Lehman College composition courses. In looking at the full archive, we investigate three features that emerged from these twenty-first-century student samples. First, freewriting makes contact with individual background knowledges. Second, freewriting places these individual knowledges into the shared vocabulary of a classroom. Third, freewriting integrates the collective background knowledges, inscribing background knowledge of students into course content, into the institution, and into the intellectual history of the academy. In sum, freewriting became a genre of localized belonging, foregrounding cultures and literacies in the ongoing list that is collective culture. And it became part of a tradition of building a commons from contact composition practices.

But I am getting ahead of myself. When I sat down in that English 111 classroom, these features had not yet gathered to form a collective. And my research goal was not to trace a tradition. Rather, my goal in the classroom was to observe a general education curriculum and to codify learning outcomes. That goal changed, in part, because the act of writing alone together changes us and changes the academy. I turn to these acts of transformation now, by returning to the artifacts of the classroom.

* * *

On that second day of my first semester as a student-researcher, I entered the classroom with two students; we hovered near the door for a few minutes, figuring out a place to go. The students who had already arrived angled their seat-desk combinations to face the front, but not quite directed forward. This gave the room the appearance of being more crowded than it was. No one seemed to notice me when I walked in. Prof D sat on the desk in a version of the outfit she'd wear for every class—loose jeans, a button down, a blazer, and Doc Martens. We had planned that I would introduce myself to the class at the end of this period. I tried to catch her attention, but she didn't register my entrance.

Several students then came in and moved around the room, arranging bags and jackets around the chairs, only to pack up again in search of another seat. Just before 11:00 a.m., three more classmates came in and, like me, stood off to the side. When we did decide on the right spot, we dropped our stuff on the desk and floor. But we sat upright, legs extended to keep in touch with our backpacks. It was a posture familiar to seasoned subway riders. On a packed train, you want to stake out personal space but not commit to fully settling in. It's important to be ready for a quick exit when the train cars open.

Seven minutes into the official start of class time, the professor faced us and began talking. "It's common to be stuck. But please do start writing," she said. Then she picked up one of the handouts that I described Xavier referring to earlier. She said this was a collection of some of the freewrites turned in the week before. It was one page of single-spaced paragraphs, numbered but not named. We could refer to these if we wanted ideas, but didn't have to.

Five students took out laptops. I grabbed my spiral notebook. A few classmates picked up the handout. Many had fallen to the floor and now served as scrap paper for four students' freewrites. Soon, a timer went off. We wrote. A fifteen-minute timer went off again. We finished. Then students were asked to form groups to read their work, for the first and only time of the term. Most stayed still, but Xavier, once again, broke the silence. He flipped his chair around and gestured to me and to two students sitting near me, Kammie and Ashley. We would each read parts of our freewrites aloud. But before that we would introduce ourselves.

Xavier identified as an adult transfer student, Black, male, thirty years old at the time of the research project, a father of two, a manager at Target, and a leader in his church. Xavier chose his research alias and signed all his informal writing this way. Kammie, who wanted to be referred to as a "later on in years teenager," was born and grew up in Pakistan and had been a resident of the Bronx since she was fifteen years old. Caretaker to three young sisters, Kammie babysat most evenings for family or friends. She said she wasn't sure what her last name would be by summer; she was getting married and hadn't decided what to do about that. So she preferred "Kammie." Ashley, who was twenty-three, described herself as "bilingual"; part Dominican, part Irish; and "a driver." The "driver" category mattered to Ashley. She didn't want me to use her last name but told me to include details about her commute and her car "situation," which I will. For now, I share the three freewrites, bolding the phrases that appeared often in the collection.

Xavier:

What I was considering writing is not what I will write about here. I was thinking about what I said last year, in that letter I wrote to my community, and also in one paper for the writing class I had to take for the engineering program. So you know, what about this **list of writing**? Well we're going to have to get on that, **gather** our **belongings** to get focused if it will continue, if it will **find a fit**, move from here to here. Because that list, it lingers in the air and can last. Thank you.

Kammie:

Was thinking about what writing I've done and what I want you to know. But what I want to say to you is that I remember the papers I did for my introductory writing class, while I was **still** working out college application essays for other schools. And I remember writing them late at night, freewriting as emails to my friends who moved abroad or got to move away from home . . . we've got all this work **left over** and here we are.

Ashley:

Are we back writing? Still stuck on that piece of writing we did last week. Well all right, let's **return**, see what's next for us. I hope this is not dragging because now I'm sitting with this other thing I wrote, and need to make connections between this and everything still, still here. That is the way it seems to be with Carman Hall classes. You will keep circling around, **returning** and running into things, and stuff. This makes me remember how to get in and out of these hallways.

The group talk lasted fifteen minutes. We chatted about words we liked from our samples. Kammie said that "list of writing" and "find a fit" were great expressions. Xavier was eager to concur. He used this phrase in class and in his writings going forward, as did a dozen other students, who would refer to the freewriting handout this way. Ashley highlighted Kammie's phrase "left over," and I appreciated Ashley's discussion of Carman Hall, which we all agreed was the ugliest, most convolutedly built structure on campus. After introductions, Xavier wanted me to read my letter first. I first told the group about my research project and scholarship and read the IRB form, which I would do again at the end of that first class period. Kammie was nonplussed that I was a professor. Xavier was interested, but less in my teaching than in my training as a PhD student, which came up in my freewrite. Here are two lines from that opening writing.

> I was wary of freewriting, though I use it often as a writer and teacher . . . still I wonder if I can think about it or do it without hearing all the critiques of the activity and the ambivalence I still feel about it, though right now I need it.

I told the group that my "wariness" had to do with a scholarly debate about process genres and with my interest in critical pedagogy. Then I provided a ten-second version of social constructivism and the myth that we can ever be "free" from constraints in writing or in any other activity. "Well, of course," was Kammie's response. She thought I was making too much of something simple ("not the first time someone told me that," was my response, which got a laugh). But I wanted to explain, so I gave some background.

I detailed how I was introduced to freewriting by two mentors, Peter Elbow and Pat Belanoff; we had used their textbook *A Community of Writers* in my practicum for first-time teachers. While in graduate school, I had worked as a teacher of writing, a writing center tutor, and then a full-time writing center administrator. In these first days as a writing studies scholar, I was taught that freewriting was a technique that would help make sense of my experience. I mentioned another mentor of mine, Min-Zhan Lu. Lu was not someone I knew personally. But her scholarship on language and politics, and her critique of "experience" pedagogies had inspired my interest in cultural and rhetorical theory.[1] Ashley thought this was all interesting but a bit off-topic. We had to keep reading the freewrites, she reminded us. So, Kammie read her sample, then Ashley. Then we turned in our samples and turned back to the lesson for the day, "features of a narrative essay."

Years later, I went back to the notes from this discussion, reading them alongside the artifacts. And I considered them in the context of century-old composition practices. Looking at what was produced in these classrooms as part of that commons tradition shows how our group was beginning to build a theory of background knowledge. Our theory was not part of the class syllabus, nor would it be registered as relevant to most course curricula. That's because we were conjuring background knowledge from work in writing.

We've seen how definitions of background knowledge were critical to the general education movement. Background knowledge came from reading "heritage texts" or accumulating the "information" that everyone "needs to know." It would give students a shared past so they can bind together for a prosperous future. In chapter 1, we saw how the SLAI educators felt confined by both the progressive and liberal-humanist definitions of background knowledge as something acquired. The SLAI wanted students to form collectives from their encounters with background knowledges as formed in contact composition. Contact composition was Louise Noyes's term for low-stakes practices we now associate with freewriting. We recall that Noyes was a world literatures teacher-research in the Stanford Language Arts Investigation; she, like Alvina Treut Burrows, Holland D. Roberts, and Walter V. Kaulfers, had recognized the coming "informal age" of communication when radio, television, and multiple kinds of discourse were becoming more readily available. They believed in courses that integrate these forms. And they wanted the "new" learner of the age—those attending their public high schools and colleges—to be authors of the emerging "cultural material." If the goal of general education was to acculturate students to common knowledge, then the goal of contact composition was to expand what knowledges count as material for the commons.

That is the kind of collective knowledge I explore in the freewrites discussed in this chapter. In order to appreciate this quality of freewriting, we need to rethink background knowledge as it has been understood in contemporary composition. Once we reorient where background knowledge comes from, we can see what it is and how it forms in writing lists made in classrooms.

FREEWRITING FOREGROUNDS BACKGROUND KNOWLEDGE

Background knowledge is a central part of the reading commons idea of the university. But it's also critical for research and teaching in writing studies; it is the information and skills students come into the class already possessing. Having background knowledge in writing and knowing what to do with that knowledge is considered essential to academic growth and success.

Background knowledge includes the experiences we've had in past schooling, the books we read before formal learning, and the skills we've acquired. All of this matter fluctuates as we move through college and life. As Min-Zhan Lu describes, background knowledge is the "often complex and sometimes conflicting templates of languages, englishes, discourses, senses of self, visions of life, and notions of one's relations with others and the world" (2004, 28). Genre theorist Charles Bazerman echoes this view, writing that when we "travel to new communicative domains, we construct our perception of them beginning with the forms we know" (Bazerman 1997, 19). Genre knowledge helps us build on the forms we know and adapt to new ways of knowing and communicating. Travel metaphors abound in studies of writing transfer. Mary Jo Reiff and Anis Bawarshi's research on first-year composition courses show that introductory college composition students tend to be "boundary crossers" or "boundary guarders." They question and repurpose their prior knowledge or stick with certainty about their genre knowledge, "regardless of task" (Reiff and Bawarshi 2011, 314). The ability to cross boundaries is essential to "highroad" transfer, which enables writing success in college and beyond (Reiff and Bawarshi 2011, 329). In order to achieve highroad transfer, students need to "make use of prior knowledge and practice" in three ways, by "drawing on," "reworking," and "creating new knowledge and practices" for themselves (Robertson, Taczak, and Yancey 2012).

Compositionists describe how many first-year students struggle to draw on their background knowledge, especially in academic writing. Some educators fault high schools for not providing enough writing in their curricula. We have learned a great deal from accounts of the testing culture of high school and how secondary education's focus on literary genres adds to students' "absence" of prior composition knowledge (Robertson, Taczak, and Yancey 2012). The "reading culture" at most high schools contributes to a lack of a "rhetorical view of both reading and writing" (Robertson, Taczak, and Yancey 2012).

Obtaining a rhetorical view—an understanding of audience, purpose, and context—is considered a vital purpose of higher learning. A rhetorical view and critical thinking were two outcomes for English 111, and the reason why the course assessed only academic genres. Many first-year composition instructors teach with informal writing activities, but don't count them in curricular documents. "Mutt genres," as Elizabeth Wardle puts it, do not do the work of rhetoric. They are forms that do not belong to any particular discipline, audience, or purpose and thus can't promote transfer (2009). An example of a mutt genre might be the commonly assigned "narrative" or "argument" paper written for no particular audience or situation. Telling a story about something is not the same as making a claim for a particular audience in a particular modality. And an argument for argument's sake is not a real genre either. As literacy theorists have long argued, all writing is "instrumental, transactional, and rhetorical" (Petraglia 1995, 80). Writing happens in genres, not in "general" practices "that do not respond to rhetorical situations requiring communication in order to accomplish a purpose that is meaningful to the author" (Wardle 2009, 777).

Meaningful purpose accomplished through close-reading skills and real genre knowledge: this nicely summarizes the goals of our English 111 assignments. The curriculum represented the belief that writing just for "practice" or to serve an "expressive" function does not serve a rhetorical purpose or a knowledge function (Beaufort 2007, 154). The narrative and argument essays assigned for the class were geared to particular audiences, with final drafts conforming to genre and mode expectations, studied at length. Prof D encouraged freewriting and reflective letters but not as content and competencies. The intention was to keep freewriting away from the knowledge that mattered to the course.

My research found that freewriting refused this distance. The artifacts situated the background knowledges of students in this class and community. I see this evidenced in three ways. First, the freewrites consistently use the past tense. Every sample collected at the start of the semester opens in the past, and so do in more than 50 percent of the samples written throughout the term. The most common phrase students employed to open freewrites was the same as I used in my sample: "I was." From here, most students moved to describe the present act of composing, defining their world as freewriters. Kammie's example was typical: "Was thinking about writing I've done . . . what I want you to know." That move, from individual past to assertion of present composing, occurred in every sample.

Second, the freewrites seek out a reader; the pronouns "we" or "us" are used in 90 percent of the samples. Ashley's example illustrated this pattern: "Well alright, let's return, see what's next for us." We observe here how students moved from the past and "I" to a "we." Xavier's example was typical: "What I was considering . . . Well we're going to have to get on that, to gather." Another version of this came from two dozen students who began with "I was not sure what to write about" and ended with "we will write about." The act of writing produced a collective engagement with writing.

Third, the freewrites connect the past and present, the moment of composing, linking background knowledge as something that enables belonging. Freewriting is often described as benefiting "future writing," not the "immediate" scene of composing (Elbow 1973, 11). Yet these samples resist movement from one place to another. They engage the past and the future to grapple with a certain presence and bring it to the course atmosphere. Let's see what these particular presences look like. Xavier's opening freewrite referenced the writing he had done as a community and religious leader and as an engineering student. For Kammie, this freewrite began with a list of the other writing she's done in the past and how that writing differentiates her from others, from those who were able to "move away from home" for college. Ashley's sample opens by looking back to the previous week's freewrite. Since she had not been absent on the first day of classes, Ashley had done that writing and was "stuck" there, "still," even though this new piece of writing had prompted a recognition of the challenges of the college infrastructure. From recognition of the recent past, of being "stuck," Ashley conjures a reader, the "you" of the sample, and offers a warning about the complex architecture of the building. Remembering how to navigate in and through academia is part of this writing. There is the "left over" work Kammie describes and the way that what is left behind travels with us. Connecting in and across time is part of the activity of these freewrites, which Ashley describes in her account of "circling" Lehman's Carman Hall and Xavier names a "list" that "lingers," which matter for the "we" called up in each of these samples.

The background knowledges we just discussed from this sample are not, on the whole, skills learned in high school. Students don't go from high school to first year to new contexts in the linear fashion assumed in much of the transfer research. Though called "first-year" composition students, at Lehman, 75 percent of the students transfer from community college, a statistic that is double the national average, although the rate of transfer at all public, nonselective colleges is increasing each year.[2] Students who are not designated as transfers are often older than eighteen, have worked during and after high school, and, in many cases, don't go directly to college, sometimes taking college courses part-time for years before enrolling. These are "first-years" but not at all new to college or composition. In the two sections of English 111 in which I enrolled, 50 percent of the students were over twenty-one, 70 percent worked full-time and wrote at their jobs, and 48 percent had taken a different writing course before this one.[3]

The situation of my study echoes the context of so many situations where students learn in what scholars call a condition of "mobility." A mobility context takes into account many transnational and local forms of transformation, circulation, and conditions, including the way texts, ideas, cultures, languages, institutions, students, literacies, and capital move in our time (Horner et al. 2021, 3). In my first semester as a student researcher, it took three weeks until Prof D had twenty-five students committed to her section; in the second semester it took twelve days. Once a complete roster was solidified, it was challenging to get students to meet out of class. Most of the students reported staying on campus only for the duration of their classes, commuting between home and caretaking responsibilities. The others said they remained on campus to print documents or use the library.

Researchers are paying attention to mobility as a material condition of learning. Literacy scholars study mobility contexts not only to adjust or accommodate these situations but to contribute to new social systems and ideologies in education. One example is Brice Nordquist's *Literacy and Mobility*. Nordquist's study addresses the material conditions of high school and college students who, like the undergraduates at Lehman, attend school while they work, travel long distances to school, and can have compromised housing conditions. His ethnography makes visible how educational mechanisms, like the time school starts or the state of public transportation, create "mobility systems" that enable, manage, predict, and constrain educational attainment for students in poor or working-class neighborhoods (Nordquist 2017, 114). The study explores objects and signs put up around high school hallways, such as banners and motivational posters, to illustrate how the institution directs students toward particular paths to "college and career readiness." Such paths don't always meet up with the direction that students' lives are taking at that time.

The pedagogical approach taken by Prof D tried to take into account the mobile lives of students. Like many other CUNY instructors, she adopted her syllabus and assignments to account for the material lives of the class community, while they were in school and out. She repeated the same freewriting prompt over and over again, especially at the start of the term, because she knew that students, like me, would be absent for the first week or two. She had revised her courses while spending a year as a faculty fellow in Lehman's Writing Across the Curriculum program, influenced by pedagogues who stressed flexibility in assignment deadlines, easy access to course materials, and a "flipped classroom" approach to course content. While a student-researcher in the course, I recognized Prof D's strategy of repetition and open access from my time teaching in these workshops. Here we stressed "backwards design," or working from course outcomes and learning goals and then considering the content and assignments for the course.[4] Most college syllabi build up to big assignments, starting off slow, picking up the pace at midterm, and culminating in substantial assessments like final exams, projects, or term papers. Prof D scaffolded assignments and syllabi, accounting for false starts like late registration and changing work schedules. Considering assessments and outcomes from the start keeps the big picture of the course in mind and makes that big picture visible and tangible to students.

In addition to these pedagogies, some faculty and activists at CUNY—who, along with Prof D, were involved in the Pathways general education curriculum—had been fighting against austerity measures in budgets that lead to unjust hiring practices and last-minute student registration. The WAC program encouraged faculty to teach the history of CUNY students and scholars protesting for labor equity, admissions reform, and basic needs that contribute to education, such as day care centers and food banks on campuses. Many Lehman teachers draw ideas from CUNY scholarship such as the longitudinal study of student writers at City College conducted by Marilyn Sternglass (1997), the College of Staten Island professor Matt Brim's (2020) analysis of how queer studies works at underfunded urban schools, and the translanguaging research of Lehman College's Cecilia Espinosa (Ascenzi-Moreno and Espinoza 2021).

These pedagogical models influenced Prof D's approach to freewriting. But to realize this genre's work in building a commons, adopting a student-centered, mobility-attuned teaching strategies is only a start. We must also recognize how mobility makes for new forms of knowledge and new social bonds, consistency, and shared experience. To do that, we must think about freewriting not as "mere" practice but as radical, content-driven practice. That is, we need to think of freewriting as a genre that inscribes background knowledges as they move.

I opened this chapter by describing how I came into English 111 one week late. Like other students, I was nervous about catching up. But I also knew that the consequences for my absences were not the same as for the students; as a researcher I had "insider status" and knowledge about how to navigate the academy, and course assessments would not affect my place as a professor (Canagarajah 2002, 168). Yet in looking at the freewriting samples, we notice that none of them represents success or achievement or insider status in the course. The freewriting did not let us catch up; it carried us onward from where we were.

Freewriting is that contact in and over time. It is "left over" and "finds a fit." It "gathers." It is one of the "belongings" of the course. It is "still" engaged with background, but also moving on, poised somewhere in between "returning and running into things." What these expressions tell us is that freewriting documents the tension that comes when we compose in time and out of routine and in the communion with others. It can't be acquired for mastery or accumulated for transfer. It is not a measure of absence but an account of pasts as they shift the atmosphere of the present. In the next section we will see how this works over the course of the term.

FREEWRITING MOVES TO FIND PLACE, FORM, EVENT

At the halfway point of the semester, I bumped into Ashley outside of Carman Hall. She waved to me as I sidestepped the city bus crossing Goulden Avenue, the street that faces the English department classrooms. Ashley and I often found each other on the way to class, as we were the only students who drove to campus rather than take public transportation. After a few weeks of what we thought had been chance meetings, we realized we were coming from the same place. Ashley dropped her niece off at a pre-K center in Kingsbridge, located a few miles from Lehman and a few blocks from the daycare where I dropped my daughter most mornings. We'd often check in about traffic patterns and parking issues.

That late October 2012 morning, I had just left the English department after visiting with colleagues. The third floor of Carman Hall is where our class met during most weeks of the term. But on this day, we were scheduled in the computer lab, located in a building added onto the original structure of that building. There are four entrances to Carman Hall. Two of the doors take you to the original architecture, built in the late 1960s and early 1970s, and two doors take you to the building's extension, constructed in the late 1990s and early 2000s. They don't always connect. Sometimes the doors are hallways that just end, sometimes you take a wrong turn and end up in an air shaft. The labyrinth architecture of Carman Hall matters here, because it is the backdrop for the second set of freewrites and the shared vocabulary and connections made in these samples.

"Are we back writing?" Ashley asked me, slipping off her headphones. I didn't have a chance to answer but liked the phrase "back writing." It was familiar, but I wasn't placing it. In fact, it was a phrase she used in the first freewrite, briefly discussed in the last section. But for the moment, I just jotted the phrase in my research notebook. And we kept walking and talking.

I learned that Ashley was deciding between two majors, either Business Administration or Forensic Science. She studied the latter subject on Saturdays at John Jay College of Criminal Justice, another CUNY campus. Ashley worked in Brooklyn and drove between schools and home and her niece's daycare in the Bronx. How to remember the best ways to navigate through the city and the pathways of this campus building came up often. We see that in her first freewriting. Returning, running, and circling, then, are conditions of composing, embedded into how Ashley writes and learns. It remains an ongoing, complex, and composing practice. "Back again" was a way to realize the power of freewriting.

Back again was also a way to describe my autoethnographical research in English 111. After some time away from the archives, I was coming back to first-year composition, but in a new way, and coming in and out of Carman Hall carrying different identities. That's a phrase I'd return to many times in this research and again here, as a way to consider free-writing as content of the course and institution. Let's look at Ashley's sample again.

> Are we **back writing**? **Still stuck** on that piece of writing we did last week. Well all right, let's return, see what's next for us. I hope this is not drag-ging because now I'm sitting with this other thing I wrote, and need to make connections between this and everything still, still here. That is the way it seems to be with Carman Hall classes. You will keep **circling around, returning and running** into things, and stuff. This makes me remember how to get in and out of these hallways.

I coded this freewrite in 2014 and categorized it as a foreshadowing of the slump that comes after a few weeks of the term. The workload in English 111 was heavy and can "drag." But when I reread the freewrites during the pandemic, while the college was still closed and I hadn't seen students face-to-face in months, I found my attention turned to other verbs, to "running" and "remember." In the early phase of my research, I thought of these freewrites in relation to the outcomes of one general education reform. When I encountered these texts again, I saw them reaching back to an old idea of the university in order to form a new writing society.

Charles Bazerman describes genres as "forms of life." In studying the emergence of forms of life, we also study interactions and "frames for social action" (1997, 19). Scholars study and teach literary and cul-tural genres, like novels or political speeches, in order to understand how social action happens in context and discourse. Emerging genres help us get a sense of what the future may be. Much of the classroom research on first-year composition genres looks at how learners transfer their writing knowledge of argument or research, for example, to other courses or the workplace. We are interested in genres that evolve in our presence, not so much to understand the past but so that we can get a grasp on what's next for communication and culture (Russell 2016, 84). However, in the artifacts I study here, we see how freewriting reaches back to the past and forward to the future in the moment of composing. And that move does not predict the future. Rather it makes writing an event. This is an event that places students in the situation of culture and knowledge-making. These freewrites make "contact" between the individual student's background knowledge and course content and then connect these parts of the past to the present. They are genres of the commons.

In the early 1990s, the editors of the only monograph devoted to freewriting hoped to reconsider this activity as a genre and an event. At this point, many composition scholars had turned away from the practice, as part of a larger critique of the writing process movement and its status in the field. But the editors of *Nothing Begins with N* (1991) argued that freewriting was more than a feature of a paradigm or a pedagogical exercise. It was a "central event" for making meaning and communicating with its own literature (Belanoff, Elbow, and Fontaine 1991, xi)

In Ashley's freewrite, and in the samples I discuss here, I see part of that literature of event-forming. Freewrites concretize what geographer Tim Cresswell (2006) calls the "metaphysics" of movement. Movement happens even when we are in confined spaces, like classrooms. Ashley's phrase "being stuck" helps us define the kind of contact made in freewriting and how we readers of this freewriting can understand it as serving a critical knowledge function in today's academy. Being stuck often implies emptiness or unproductivity. But in the case of these texts, and in Ashley's sample, *stuck* expresses composing through complex conditions: students have arrived with their longer or local pasts and the background knowledges they came into class already having or those generated in the class; they will not necessarily leave them as they transfer to another course.

"I define mobility in terms of inequality," writes Rebecca Lorimer Leonard. Leonard documents the importance of distinguishing between free-floating "flexible" descriptions of movement and the kind of movement that controls and contains (2021, 68). Coding for patterns, as I did in the first round of this research, did not account for the uneven and nonlinear realities of language-shifting in student forms. A 2022 survey of CUNY students found that close to 40 percent reported being "housing insecure." One in five CUNY students dealt with some form of food insecurity, as a 2019 report reveals. Nearly 50 percent of students dealt with some form of food insecurity over a thirty-day period. These numbers are higher for women and for women with children and are certain to rise because of the pandemic.[5] The definition of "housing insecure" doesn't include people experiencing homelessness, which was 14 percent of the CUNY student body in 2019. Other situations students face are not always counted in this data, like the need to live with families in single-family spaces, the cost of childcare, and the challenge of paying more than 50 percent of income on rent.[6]

In student writing, statistics like these are fleshed out and folded into scenes of learning, something I realized in reading these artifacts years after they were produced in response to one classroom prompt. Nedra Reynolds, Mary Jo Reiff, and other rhetorical theorists imagine genre as both "movement and dwelling" (Reiff 2016, 115), and their research explores how we use language and how it uses us (Reynolds 2004, 46). Mobility demands "adaptability," writes Christine Donahue, and that means movement and staying still happen together; this is something more complex than "transfer" (Donahue 2021, 17). The freewriting here is not walled off from the content and culture of the class. Rather it is a "central" meaning-making activity, a way to find contact and connection in the local academic environment (Belanoff, Elbow, and Fontaine 1991, xi). Freewriting makes that movement available as an epistemological event.

Below are three more examples of movement as it manifests into forms of knowledge and belonging in the academy. Bolded are the phrases and pronouns that appeared, with slight variation, in 70 percent or more of the archive at weeks two and seven of the semester:

1. **What others wanted to know** about my writing is that I wrote a lot in my high school days and years between high school and college in creative journals, about my identity and politics as a multiracial new immigrant to America, I don't know why but that helps me as I think about if **we** need so much of that kind of writing time now we're experienced.

2. **Loved freewriting**, so easy. I have done it 1000 times but don't have a record. You should see the application letters and personal statements I wrote for college admissions—never got to go to these schools but that's for another freewrite. But going back to that time, I don't know, now **we** might be finding it hard, painful even, to slow down and look at these words. Maybe those will mysteriously find their way on the list or some other list we're doing over these four-something years?

3. **I was not sure** what to write at first. Maybe this trouble I am having is because of a lack of writing experience, having mostly taken engineering

courses in high school and technical college. I am from Jamaica by the way and have lived here for five years. I am looking at the syllabus and **we** are likely wondering if this writing will be part of the other kinds of writing due as indicated there. There's the science writing and the structured writing I did back in my home country, so there is a lot to do here at college.

The freewrites in this group were unsigned and none of the authors described their intentions. This leaves us with a few options of how to understand the artifacts. We can see them as typical reactions to the classroom assignment. Most classroom writing prompts "choreograph" time and uptake for students, who respond with predictability: read the assignment, perform the task, wait to be assessed, react to the standard situation (Bawarshi and Reiff 2010, 91). Each one of these samples follows the assignment situation to write for fifteen minutes, and many follow standard patterns. One such pattern is the use of language that describes how students are "not sure" about what to write. This can be found in sample three, as well as in half of the artifacts. That language confirms Hannah Rule's study that freewriting is not an easy task for students, though many describe it as such (2013).

Yet there are other approaches to exploring these writing samples. In the last section, we looked at freewrites for their focus on the past. In this group, we see how freewrites, read as a group, show a pileup of the pasts. One individual's private, personal declaration of movement through time and space is part of a larger, collective work of freewriting. The professor's pedagogical approach, to make what Xavier called the "list" of writing visible on the course website, helps us notice this collective pattern. We can also note the collective content of freewrites and treat these texts as aggregate artifacts, or what the SLAI called "cultural material." For example, in sample one, the student writes creatively in a journal about the politics and identity concerns related to being a multiracial person and a new immigrant. This is the impetus to make the move from the past of writing into the present of the classroom, as an "experienced writer." "Loved freewriting" opens sample two, indicating a past relationship with this genre that allows it to become something new, something made in this classroom, in this composing moment, with these classmates: "Now we might be finding it hard, painful even." Not being "sure" about what to write about first allows details about the past to emerge for sample three, including how being "from Jamaica" and "having mostly taken engineering courses" leads this student to ground himself and his "freewriting" into the course syllabus. Fifteen students detail some aspect of their lives that might be considered a lack or "absence" of prior or background knowledge. In sample three, the student's experience taking engineering courses is framed as something that limits their wider understanding of knowledge. However, the sample then moves to a question about the syllabus and class requirements. That question is also an assertion of what being from Jamaica and a "science thinker" can bring to the work of this writing class, to the college, and to what sample two notes as the "list" that may form in "four-something" years of academic work. This pattern—from what's missing in a student's background to how they could belong in the class—is found in 80 percent of the samples.

Understanding what is absent from the past is necessary. It is a resource, not only to find skills or knowledge for the future but to be present in the composing community of this classroom and its work engaging the individual backgrounds of students. This idea was first explored in the late 1930s research of Alvina Treut Burrows. She analyzed hundreds of freewrites written by students ranging from elementary school to graduate school. She found no common theme among the artifacts she studied. The content of the freewrites varied, depending on the context and teacher prompt. However, what she did find about freewrites is that when this writing was read together (she called this a "stockpile"), the material represents a "break" in the experience of school. That break could be integrated into the content of the class, if researchers and students see this work as a course goal (Burrows, Jackson, and Saunders 1939, 187–227).

Recall that the prompt for this composition classroom asked English 111 students to write about "anything you want." We can't know if the topics students wrote about are what they wanted or felt compelled to write about. And students didn't assume their work would be returned. We can, however, notice how students negotiate the space-time constraints of this assignment—fifteen minutes—to construct histories and create communities, to find each other in that time-space of the course and the college. Once the past is named, it can be called on to be something else and, further, for students to be something else alongside others.

I close this section by returning to the discipline of writing studies and its approach to background knowledge, transfer, and content. We have looked at the way freewriting performs mobility. That feature was noticed decades ago, in research that helps me see how collective forms of mobility contribute to the way students engage background knowledges and belong to the classroom, to its content, and to the institution.

In a 1980s study of freewriting, Richard Haswell recorded some surprising findings. He didn't expect to find common features and a shared organization in his collection of student samples. The study recognized that the way students freewrite often depends on how they are prompted to do so by the instructor. But Haswell noted that the paradoxes of open-ended prompts—write what you want, but do so constrained by the clock, the assignment, and the institutional power dynamics—produced some unique discourse. His research found that among about a hundred free-writes, students mixed forms and styles and, most importantly, rerouted a reader's habitual ways of interpretation. If students are assigned an argumentative essay for a particular course, they follow the genre and rhetorical modes of that course or that discipline. Teachers read and assess according to the way students enact the rules of those modes. But when students freewrite, students follow guidelines set by the community; freewriting creates the condition for what Haswell called "situational organization." Readers encountering a body of freewriting work can seek out the situational organization of this literature. That practice can render a particular world, a temporary world society of writers.

Haswell had his doubts about situational organization. He wondered if the content and skills produced from this genre were, in the end, "gratuitous" (Haswell 1991, 51). I want to think about gratuitous information as the very event of a writing classroom, the rigorous, raw material of the commons. Haswell defined "situational organization" as a form of "metadiscourse," or discourse about discourse (48). Genre theorist Janet Giltrow unpacks the role of metagenres. They are "situated language about situated language," uniquely suited to provide commentary on the situation. Metagenres are often found "hovering near" the real genre (Giltrow 2002, 195), the study guide that accompanies a textbook, for example (191). The hyphen in her use of the term signals how Giltrow thinks of this genre. It is a way to mediate between process and product, between general and specialized, between primary and second-ary genres. Anis Bawarshi summarizes Giltrow's findings: "Genres such as manuals and handbooks provide shared background knowledge and guidance in how to produce and negotiate genres and genre uptakes within genre sets and systems" (2016, 45).

Shared background knowledge is hard to codify or quantify. Indeed, Giltrow calls this knowledge "atmospheres surrounding genres" (2002, 195). As we learned from Alvina Burrows, atmospheres made in writing can be "elusive" (Burrows, Jackson, and Saunders 1939, 174). Atmo-spheres are everywhere, but we are not always conscious of our experi-ence in or with them. While such metagenres don't necessarily function exactly in the way intended or prompted, they call into being new kinds of practices and communities. Writers understand and interact with metagenres in a variety of ways, and these in turn alter reception of the primary genres. We cannot assume that common knowledge or belonging are certain or even likely features or uptakes of freewriting. However, we can consider freewriting a genre and note when and how it comments on and constructs academic connection and community.

Rhetorical genre theorists provide examples of metagenres doing this work. Dylan B. Dryer shows how ordinary citizens create new genres by reacting to official documents, like reports on rezoning or urban planning. His research reveals how responses are forms of civic writing and can help in "developing solidarity" (Dryer 2016, 71). Solidarity is not sameness but instead is unity by situation, through a group's common interests, objectives, and standards collected in the shared practice of writing. As the SLAI put it in 1942, solidarity is a "prerequisite to success" in education (Kaulfers, Kefauver, and Roberts 1942, 396).

The SLAI researchers did not find solidarity among their fellow scholars. But we might find some solidarity for their beliefs here, in these freewrites. Claiming freewriting as a form of solidarity or belonging means allowing alternative structures of ideas into the university. Sara Ahmed has argued for attending to such alternative structures. To teach, learn, and expand background knowledges that matter to culture, we need to get better at seeing, remembering, and codifying contributions of the often undervalued. In the opening of *On Being Included* (2012), Ahmed recalls a time she was made to feel out of place in her own neighborhood, dismissed and then discarded, after police officers stopped to question her presence because she is not white and because there had been some burglaries in her town. To remember that experience, Ahmed explains, and to do the work of remembering the individual histories and experiences of those who inhabit the places where we live and study, is essential. It helps reorient attention from the abstract ideal of collective to the actual. Belonging has to be insisted upon in situations and forms organized and repeated as part of the fabric of an institution. And it needs to involve the very people who have been excluded or defy the usual ways of doing things.

The usual way of doing this is to reform curricula and curate reading lists. But there are other ways we form worlds. Informal writing by students requires that scholars and teachers turn their attention to writing, a "political reorientation" (Ahmed 2012, 1) that does not guarantee certain outcomes but attends to the processes of emergent connections. In the freewriting studied here, knowledge and culture are transferred *in* the act of writing to the time and place of the present and realized in the communal space of composing. Freewriting pays attention to the discursive background knowledges and literacies of the public academy. And it temporarily connects students to each other and to the course, the institution, and the ongoing act of making the new content for the university.

FREEWRITING INSCRIBES CONTENT

In the last weeks of the semester in English 111, we were preparing for the outgoing, final assessment, an in-class argumentative essay based on a short article given out in advance of exam day. During weeks thirteen and fourteen of the two semesters, we would freewrite for the last time. We followed the same prompt but did not meet in writing groups to share our work. The freewrites were not collected by the professor (only for the research), and I assumed that most of us would write about what we would do next, after the term ended. Discourse about the future is evident in the samples discussed below. But the most obvious feature here is discourse about the past. In the artifacts analyzed earlier, we saw how freewrites engendered a return to the past as part of belonging to the time and place of the course. That time and place was inscribed in the act of composing, in the freewrite. The freewrites here also begin in the past, and travel through these histories in order to find their footing in the academy. Here are a few examples:

1. Past the first big essay and what I was going to talk about here or mark and now relating to the work coming due (including an evaluation at my job, the reading due). I remember this journal that's halfway filled, something I started doing years ago when I lived with family in the D.R. I am now asking how the random parts **find a fit**, how reading **returns** and the rest **remains**—that is still unknown.

2. Was thinking about this morning. I was tired. Just like my kids are . . . busy too and still **stuck** with this writing from a few weeks ago (graded but it's with me). I'm taking four classes and all of them require some paper at this point. I was wondering about that on my train ride here. I directed someone where to go, she didn't speak English I don't think, but needed to know about the last stop and I could tell her that by pointing though someone took over in Spanish, another Lehman student actually. I see this tiredness as taking care of others and also **translating** what we're doing with this **list of writing** which is moving with the next thing.

3. We wondered about this for a while. We wanted to know what we wanted others to know about us as writers for a while now and am not sure at this point what **remains**, what additional information this **list of writing** could offer us though I am writing about that teacher I wrote about, from Pakistan. So much has come up for me about that place from that paper, from the start of the semester, that's **still remaining**. I've shared that reading with family and friends.

Sample two declares that the author needs "this tiredness from taking care of others to translate to this next thing." We did not know what the "next thing" would be at week six of the term, only that it would materialize "through translation." There are two ways that the term "translation" might be understood. First, we can see how the freewrite translates the language and cultural moves made by students in academia. Throughout the informal writing collected in this research, there is a metadiscourse on the moves made by writers who identify in this class as dual or multilingual (70 percent). These texts illustrate how moving among languages "involves diverse semiotic resources and ecological affordances" (Canagarajah 2013, 6). Translation among languages also engages race and ethnicity and the racial bias in literacy approaches, like certain understandings of "code-switching." Literacy is not a switch that goes on and off. Instead, as Neisha-Anne Green argues, literacies are embodied and "intertwined" (2016, n.p.). There exists a place, this freewrite says, for investigating the translation and incorporation of these experiences into the mesh, or interdependent event, of writing.

Translation here is also a metaphor that describes the epistemological transporting that needs to be done to write and learn and remain in school while attending to the design of the institution, the body in motion, the others in the class, the "we" that returns and claims a presence in all of these samples. Each of these begins with a statement of the past and then reaches into the present composing situation: "We are writing for fifteen minutes, we are still writing even though we don't know if it will make it to the list." And then each does the work of "translating" what is individual to what is collectively "remaining" for this group of students.

Remaining is a verb of insistence and place. I read it here as a way to claim connection to college. In sample three, "remain" appears twice, once to refer to questions that linger and once as a verb meaning something like to stick around or leave a residue, to translate background knowledge, return to it, and find its fit. The writer of sample one uses "remain" and "return" to connect the parts of his writing life in the Dominican Republic and in the present and to articulate the contradictions that come when parts "still" don't "fit" into prescribed essays.

Remaining appears as a term in 60 percent of the archive. Different from the usual metrics for measuring higher education, retention and transfer, or the ability to translate skills from school to the workplace, remaining speaks to an ongoing, complex, composing practice of higher learning. Remaining is a way of being in the academy that is intimately tied to the "list of writing" described in samples two and three.

We know that students take a longer time to finish their degrees than they did just two decades ago, and often take an "uneven" path to graduation, dropping out and returning several times. The National Center for Education Statistics (NCES) defines retention rates as measuring "the percentage of first-time undergraduate students who return to the same institution the following fall" and reports that at nonselective public institutions like CUNY's Lehman College, the six-year retention rate is about 60 percent, compared with 82 percent at more selective public or private institutions.[7]

Since the early 2000s, there have been multiple efforts to improve CUNY's rate of retention. These include large-scale general education curricular reforms, like Pathways. And they include smaller-scale efforts, like teaching and learning centers, service-learning programs, and more public-oriented curricula. Yet I discovered that freewriting is a practice of remaining; it is, as Ahmed puts it, a "reorientation" of the retention and transfer measure. And it can be made to "find a fit" into the local mission and history of an institution. Freewriting conjures the particulars of how students move through the academy and among languages, jobs, and caretaking and other complex community and family responsibilities. These texts embed multiple, moving selves manifested in race, culture, gender, language, geography, and family into the idea and architecture of the academy. And freewriting marks the active work of remembering, remaining, of recommitting oneself over and over to an institution—to Lehman and CUNY—and to literacy instruction, to gathering to write in the US academy.

Samples one and three illustrate how freewrites inscribe movement of self and culture into a history of the public commons. The samples return to texts written and read in the near past. In the act of returning to old essays, and in reliving the steps taken from the past, new connections are made: between people and history. Using the freewriting prompt to return to an old assignment, the author of sample three recognizes how her perspective on the essay and on Pakistan has changed as time has passed. The freewrite enables this student to acknowledge, even though she is moving on, that background knowledge she came in with and knowledge made in the class "still remains." Understood this way, translation and remaining perform "contact."

Translation and remaining are forms of inscribing background knowledge into this classroom and into the institution; they extend the lists that count as course content and as intellectual history. Like background knowledge, belonging has a host of synonyms: inclusion, engagement, acceptance. It is often invoked in college mission statements. The

National Survey of Student Engagement (NSSE) tracks belonging in hundreds of colleges and universities, through questionnaires, surveys, and measuring student participation in clubs, events, and other campus activities. The findings shared in NSSE reports are differentiated by types of institutions, discipline of study, and different backgrounds (race, class, home nation, language). Overall, the research concludes that belonging is a sense that students can relate to others in the campus community.[8] Institutions respond to such results by engaging in general education reform, curricular revision, and community-building campus programs.

This chapter asks how the academy might respond, beyond institutional reports, to questions of belonging and solidarity. What if belonging was something we do, rather than something that is, or should be? What if belonging could not be possessed or acquired but is something to actively compose? What if forms of belonging made in the academy became part of intellectual history?

Freewriting helps to invite a flexible, rhetorical form of solidarity built by the background knowledges that students already possess and can claim for the purpose of making connections with others, to make more knowledge. Belonging is about concretizing the work of remaining as thinkers and writers in the academy, in recalling background knowledges and in the empowering act of embedding them in the writing of others.

Though the students and teachers move on from this class, the freewriting can remain as part of the cultural literacies of this institution. Xavier explains the list of freewriting that came together in this college composition class as something that "lingers in the air," a way to "gather" belongings. A list of writing enables a *return* to prior knowledge, relating that to current learning, communicative, and community experience of this classroom. In making space for these two exigencies to coexist, freewrites enact a rhetorical, ethical, often radical choice to *remain* in the classroom, in solidarity with others, and be counted as part of the foundation and purpose of the university, to be part of an ongoing list of knowledge.

This list of knowledge resonates with Charlemae Hill Rollins's call for educators to take on "responsibilities" for integrating not only diverse authors but new authors into the canon and the school system. We have seen how freewriting remembers these responsibilities. It contributes new and different background knowledges to the content of the course, inscribes kinds of belonging, and embeds these into institutional and cultural material. The next chapter asks how we can correspond with this cultural material to reconstruct the academy.

4

READING TO RECONSTRUCT

In November of 2019, members of the Latinx Student Alliance of Lehman College wrote a letter, delivered to faculty and administrators, and then shared it with the college community. It begins: "We, as the Latinx Student Alliance (LSA), would like to put our support and activism behind bringing forth more diversity in all English courses and English major/minor paths. We are reaching out to you with our goals for these changes." The letter follows up with a list of seven steps the college could take to transform the English department curriculum. These include reducing the number of mandated courses in British literature, adding a Latinx literatures requirement, implementing an interdisciplinary committee of students and teachers to consult on new curricula, hiring more professors of color, unbundling "ethnic literatures" as a single category, and amending reading requirements so that students gain access to the histories, cultures, and experiences of non-European and non-Western writers.

Over the next two years, the college reacted to the letter by reforming its English major. Here I respond to the letter by framing it in the history of the composition commons. Composed at a pivotal moment of change, this one student artifact invites us to consider local articulations of shared knowledge shift and how these contribute to the idea of the American university.

The student letter was written in 2019, when Lehman College, like many educational institutions, was reevaluating curriculum and engaging in diversity, equity, and inclusion efforts. In Lehman's English department, we were reading scholarship about the origins of the American university and its ties to slavery and settler colonialism, watching the news as campus statues at storied universities turned into protest sites, as campus statues of enslavers who built American colleges toppled to the ground.[1] And we were thinking about the courses available to students in general education.

Much of that thinking took place in faculty meetings, classrooms, hallways, and college-wide town halls. But by the end of 2019, our in-house curricular conversations had reached a larger audience. Lehman is not

https://doi.org/10.7330/9781646425433.c004

the campus media tends to cover in its CUNY beat. Usually the "flag-ship" campuses in Manhattan (City, Hunter, and Baruch College) get public attention. Yet weeks after the letter was written, talk of Lehman's English department found its way to administrative and activists' social media feeds and news outlets.[2] Two months later, the pandemic hit and the 2020 uprisings for racial justice followed. By early summer of 2020, the goals of the Latinx Student Alliance letter were understood as part of a global movement and a national crisis in American education.

In the first half of the book, we drew a pattern of history: crisis fol-lowed by reform. We noted how the meaning of and requirements for general education in America followed this pattern. The same formula works to describe the 2021 change in Lehman's English major. But Lehman's curricular overhaul happened faster than is common in academia, less than two years from receipt of the letter. That swift response is thanks to the persistence of several early-career professors in the English department, mostly women of color, who advocated for change.[3] Today, all majors are required to take Latinx Literature; African American and Black Diasporic Literatures; Research, Rhetoric, and Writing Studies; and a revised introduction to the majors course. Previously called "Introduction to Literary Studies," this requirement is now renamed "Unsettling English Studies" and centers on "English as a form of knowledge and power vis à vis race, class, gender, sexuality, ability, literacy or other axes of authority."[4]

The new curriculum upends nearly a century of British and Western literature dominance in the English department. It addresses changes in disciplinary knowledge, allows student choice, and requires atten-tion to literature and cultures ignored for decades. It also focuses on what the LSA letter called the "erased" groups of literary and cultural study—women and people of color—who comprise over 80 percent of Lehman's undergraduate population. We have come a long way.

But now we are somewhere else—months and worlds apart from where we were in 2019. As students and faculty return to the classrooms after a global pandemic, the letter and our reform resonate differently. How can we continue to read and respond to this student artifact, not only to stave away crisis but to cultivate a commons?

One approach is to consider this artifact not only as correspondence between groups of individuals but also between student writers and the academy. Four undergraduates signed this: Ariel Vargas, Rebecca Y. S. Perez, Miqueas Molano, and Lily Hooks. These writers addressed the piece to a particular person: the Dean of Arts and Sciences. And they described it as a statement about the curriculum. Yet the letter also claims its authors as a collective—the "club's community and student body"—who position the statement as "reaching out" to a "you" about timely, local, specific goals. These goals could have long-term, large, general repercussions that would initiate the "great beginnings of change" in education. In a statement sent to *Latino Rebels* after the original letter was composed, the LSA clarified the purpose of the letter. They identified the "proud" Lehman students who wrote the letter on behalf of this "minority serving institution," its "students and its borough" (*Latino Rebels* 2019). The student organization reminded readers that the list of goals were important. But they are the "least" of what is required; "individually and combined," these steps head towards another goal: for Lehman students to see "themselves as possible authors of their own texts."

When we first received the letter, faculty concentrated on following through on the seven suggestions for reform. These came in a bulleted list of points. A "demand" is how some defined these suggestions. The media outlet *Latino Rebels* tweeted out the letter with this headline: "Lehman College's Latinx Student Alliance Pens Letter Demanding Diversity in English Department Curriculum." Nowhere in the LSA letter do the authors use the term *demand*. Instead, the students present their letter as a statement. The distinction matters.

To be sure, the LSA letter is part of a tradition of college students using literacy activism to make change. And making demands is part of that. CUNY's radical open-admissions decision from the 1970s can be traced to Black and Puerto Rican student-activists and contributed to important literacy interventions at Lehman College and other CUNY campuses.[5] Yet the 2019 LSA letter, and reflective letters more generally, do something more than demand curricular change. They insist on authorship.

When the letter takes on authorship as a mission, it moves between local needs and big picture, from a list of goals to a sweeping vision. It also moves from a specific salutation of "Dear Dean of Arts and Humanities" to the general reader: "We are telling you what we would like to see in our education: a reflection of ourselves and of the world" (*Latino Rebels* 2019).[6]

What the LSA letter calls education as a "reflection of ourselves and the world," I have called the composition commons. The LSA letter is no longer in mailboxes or a topic for internet chatter. But it pulsates with continued importance, as part of this history of building shared knowledge in college and as a radically different way of creating change in the academy. To read this letter again is to consider how our core generates "great beginnings of change." Does a revision of core courses answer the call for students to become "authors" of their own texts?

There are many ways to respond to this question. Lehman's faculty took two familiar approaches. By adding Black, Latinx, Asian, and Indigenous literary traditions to our core courses, we were broadening the canon and extending the reach of "English" beyond national borders. Here we conjured the legacy of cultural literacy and its belief that a commons can be acquired through a shared reading list. Like cultural critics of the last century, we championed the ideals of a liberal education and of the humanities. The English major, we said, was a place to bring together background knowledges of our evolving, diverse, collective past. And in adding a Rhetoric and Writing core course, my colleagues and I rekindled the idea that cultural literacy happens with shared information and common competencies. We said our new course would address new habits of mind required of our diverse, global age. And we cited "culturally responsive," language justice, and anti-racist curricula, along with scholars in digital rhetoric to back up our choice to add the introduction to the major.[7] A class in cultural rhetorics, multilingual texts, and literacy studies could add to the relevance and the transferable skills acquired from the English major.

Updating courses and making reforms to curricula is important work. But it is not transformative work. Transformation requires "reflection of the world" and new authors and materials in our courses. And we need only look at student writing to find it.

In this chapter, we explore the features of reflective letters that make them transformative forms of correspondence. My first example of this kind of reflection came from the Latinx Student Alliance letter. There are differences between this letter and the kind produced in many composition courses. Written in response to classroom experiences and not a teacher prompt, the LSA letter was coauthored, went viral on social media, and was read outside of classroom walls. The reflective letters we study here are written in response to teacher prompts. Yet the two kinds of letters share patterns that run across these two archives. First, the letters ask questions about the relationship between curricular reforms and everyday experiences of moving through college, and the learning that happens in those negotiations. Second, letters challenge narrow definitions of authorship. Third, these letters offer direct instruction in how to read student correspondences reconstructively: as critical cultural material.

Reconstructive is a term I borrow from the Stanford Language Arts Investigation. The teacher-researchers saw this as a methodology that expands on "close reading." Long before our contemporary inquiry into diversity and anti-racist pedagogies, teacher-researchers offered reconstructive reading as a way to ask critical questions about who has access to important texts and intellectual capital in the academy. The SLAI encouraged "lived in letters" as a way to turn these questions into writing activities. These letters could be private or public. They letters could be student-to-student or student-to-instructor correspondence. And they were reflections on relationships built in classroom writing, connections made between objects of study and their worlds. That relationship became part of course syllabi in the SLAI, and the student letters were integrated into reading and curricular "lists." A list of writing can't be contained in reading requirements. It must be layered, addressed in parts, and reflected on. This work does not start and stop with crisis and solution. As the SLAI educators explained, it happens in "combined" acts of reading and writing, in the middle knowledge that emerges from our composing and responding to these compositions.

In the last chapter, we looked at how freewriting makes contact with the background knowledges of students and inscribes these into the content of the course and institution. When students write alone together and when teachers and scholars read this writing as literature, as material that belongs in time and transcends it, we expand the cultural material that defines intellectual work. Reflective letters build on the list of background knowledges. A reflective letter is not a policy, pedagogy, or curricular requirement. But it intervenes in the usual means of creation, reception, and delivery of knowledge in the academy.

REFLECTIVE LETTERS CORRESPOND FROM THE MIDDLE

In fall 2012 and fall 2013, English students wrote six letters over the course of the semester. All were responses to the same prompt: "Write a letter, addressed to anyone you want, about the steps you took to complete the assignment just turned in." The prompt drew from research in composition stressed in the WAC program at Lehman. As "first-person accounts," reflective letters can teach close reading of one's own writing, making "visible" the features of a text (Jung 2011, 629). Our English 111 sections, like all composition courses in CUNY's Pathways curriculum, stressed the ability to "read and listen analytically and critically" and, following the Common Core State Standards, to gain "mastery" of one's own reading and writing.[8] The professor saw the letter as a means to be "more aware" of our reading and learning habits.

In this section, we spend time with the first reflective letter written in English 111. I highlight the features of two student letters, written by members of my peer-review group. Peer groups met during class, in the week that immediately followed an assignment due date. In both semesters of my classroom research, the opening reflective letter prompt asked students to explain the steps we took to complete our first graded assignment, a narrative about an influential teacher. We had read several essays describing the teacher-student relationship and then had to write a narrative of our own, explaining the influence a teacher had on our learning.[9] Students were instructed to define influence in any way, and while we had models, we were not required to cite these published works. I quote from the two letters below.

> Dear Professor,
>   I took a few steps to write this and then a few back and then I spoke to some people who live with me about it. Some of them don't write in English, but I translated what they said and told classmates and we agreed with my relatives that I had good details and told a funny story but didn't include anything about influence. Maybe I'm saying that because I was in the middle of everything, complicated, missing closeness. This is hard to talk about. If we did this again, I'd probably change the teacher I wrote about and say something else, maybe we would find out and quote others about how influence is hard to talk about, or that we don't really believe in influence. I wrote it **parts in shifts**.
>
>   Best,
>   Adam

> Greetings,
>   Not certain if this has everything it's supposed to have, it is a strong essay, even if it's not got it all, but you all know that it is still brewing. I don't really see why I'm reflecting on the finished thing when it's not done. I mean it's done, turned in, and edited and pretty good I think. But it's still out there, drifting along. Like I said, I finished the version just in time, the one we're talking about here, in my kitchen, actually, one daughter yelping out her times tables, the other making mess with cupcakes for a bake sale and I had what was in front of me and also **interrupted memories**—about those earlier days alone in my other world—adding layers to it all the time, hoping everyone likes the final version, which I think is well not done. As I said.
>   Thank you for your attention.
>   Razie

I've highlighted two phrases that appear often in these artifacts. Adam describes shifts at work or "parts in shifts" and Razie describes ongoing caretaking situations or "interrupted memories." Of the thirty-six samples collected from this first reflective letter prompt, thirty-three had phrases depicting learning to write and learning to learn as processes of naming what happens in the breaks between writing. Other examples of such phrases include "writing in the back and forth," "the giving and taking of ideas as I thought," and "keep looking." From these phrases an idea about shared knowledge emerged, which echoes an idea gleaned from the SLAI classroom case studies. This is the way letters reform or alter curricular norms from "the middle" or from the "lived in" condition of student composing.

Focusing on the "middle"-made knowledge is something Louise Noyes of the SLAI did in her World Literatures course in 1939. There, she asked students to document the relationship between the books they read and the places they lived. Students wrote in class after time spent on trips to neighborhoods surrounding their commuter school. They visited both local landmarks and community places, bringing the world literature reading assigned for the day into these sites of personal, commercial, familial, civic, and cultural life. Students recorded their reading experiences, offering interpretations of text and place. Noyes's goals were exposure to literature and fluency with writing. She also wanted her class to think through the encounter of received and lived knowledge. While the progressive educators focused on lived experience and the literary humanists stressed close, objective readings, Noyes's approach was to stress the relationship, often a challenging one, between "lived in" learning and reading books. She saw that relationship as a step toward realizing a connection between text and self.

That relationship is illuminated in the letters explored in this section. Adam's letter was the first to appear in my archive, and I'll begin here. Like all the letters composed in English 111, Adam wrote after completion of the final assignment. His letter prompts the reader to see that assignment as both unfinished and faulty in its conception. Our assignment assumed that everyone would have an "influential" teacher to write about. Adam explains how "influence" is something that is always being translated or altered because of movement between languages, homes, work, and cultures. His sample provides personal details about his daily life followed by a statement that creates distance between the reader of his assignment (the teacher) and the writer of the letter (Adam): "It's hard to talk about." He had written an essay about a coach and tutor who inspired his interest in math and finance. But influence assumes a "belief." The reflective letter puts this assumption into a living context, connecting individuals to see if this belief holds up.

From what was hard or missing comes a statement about finding presence and fulfillment through reflection. Adam's letter begins a revision of the professor's original assignment prompt. He notes that "we" might want to write about "influence" differently, given that "parts in shifts" complicates writing lives. Adam meant parts in shifts literally; he composed the essay over ten days in eight fifteen-minute segments in the basement break room of a Midtown office building. Twenty-one at the time, he identified as white, male, a native speaker of Albanian, and the first in his family to attend college. Though registered as a full-time student, Adam worked two jobs as a security officer, a total of thirty-two hours a week, and shared a room with brothers, so he rarely studied at home. Adam was his real name; he chose not to use a last name.

Adam spoke often of his job and needing to be "all over the place," as he put it that morning. Stopping and starting the essay over many periods of time changed his product and leaves the reader unsure if it is finished. Though directed to reflect, he avoids what many critics see as a trap of process writing: the compulsion to use this discourse as "proof of learning" (Jung 2011, 643). Instead, "parts in shifts" continues, alters, and remakes the original assignment and repurposes the letter as a reflection on multilingualism and middle-made composition. The concept of "influence," for example, evolves through an examination of the shifts in his work and writing life. This artifact defines knowledge as a moving and translating entity, something hard to pin down and get close to, but emergent in the act of writing. The way Adam comes to know what he knows about influence, the way he understands his belief in relation to others, is through this reflection on the worlds of his writing. The reflective letter then might help in transferring skills and knowledge from one place to another. But its primary purpose is to be a temporary space for placing, for seeing that movement.

Scholars tell us that literacy comes to us segmented. We don't learn to read or write or reflect all at once; literacy is not acquired but rather "accumulated" and "amalgamated" from home and life and multiple other networks, communities, and languages (Brandt 1995). And it is not possible to discard literacies and knowledge learned in one arena (like school) in order to learn in another (at work, for example); there are no silos around language. Adam offers a way to concretize the work of literacy accumulation and illuminates how writing takes shape and shows its shape-shifting properties.

The year we were composing reflective letters about writing, sociologists Richard Arum and Josipa Roska's *Academically Adrift* came out to great acclaim. The book made waves by asserting that college students were learning less and working and socializing more. We recall from chapter 2 that Arum and Roska reported "widespread agreement" that the "complex and competitive" age, brought on by globalization and the digital revolution, required students to gain "individual mastery" over a range of general skills (2011, 11, 54). These skills included reading closely and attentively, without being "adrift" in the distractions of work and social life.

Adam would agree that his school work was full of disruptions, often because of his jobs. He would likely join Tony Scott, James Rushing Daniel, and other compositionists who argue for bringing labor issues to the forefront of rhetorical education. And like other CUNY students, Adam was interested in what wasn't yet a nationally discussed political position: that public college should be free.[10] But Adam also stressed the need for time to reflect on work, with others, and to use the classroom to write. Writing is labor-intensive, as scholars have shown (Brandt 2014). Adam's letter makes a space to share particular moves made in between one space and another.

Adam did not set out to comment on learning and literacy. His reflection was not read by educators or shared over social media, like the LSA letter or the book *Academically Adrift*. It is not a "performance of publics" (Reiff and Bawarshi 2016, 4). However, when Adam's letter is read next to the other letters, we see a strong picture emerging of learning in our complex age and the role that writing plays in that learning. Adam describes how his final draft is "missing closeness." Yet the reflective letter crafted that missingness into material. It is a reality of writing as we translate languages, negotiate parts in shifts of work, and remake assignments to suit how closeness is understood by students.

Reading Razie's letter alongside Adam's helps us see how this genre can communicate knowledge made in the middle. Her phrase "interruptive memories," like "parts in shifts," turns our attention as readers to writing and learning made in a moment but also among multiple temporal contexts, in between abstract thinking and fractured memories. Her letter describes the completed assignment as a product of mixing together the everyday objects of the now (the "mess with cupcakes") with the abstractions of the mind that come from experiences past and future—with memories, with expectations.

Razie's final essay was composed "just in time" though she was not a last-minute student. The final version, a lively narrative about an influential science teacher, came together way past midnight and is described as not quite right. She wonders if her essay is like others. Then she invites those others to see through the mask of official, dominant school genres, or what Linda Brodkey called the "hidden curriculum" (1996, 3). She explains how she composes her assignment in one place, in the kitchen, and also in the complexity of fractured, moving, temporary realities. The letter opens with "Greetings." Then it subtly conjures a "you," as did the Latinx Student Alliance letter. This "you" is the reader who would understand why her turned-in final essay is not finished. Her letter concretizes memories as part of the writing process and an intervention in the dominant temporal construction of higher education. And the piece defines interruptions not as a roadblock but as a resource to challenge the constructions of knowledge created by due dates, assignments, and curricular outcomes.

Razie transferred to Lehman the previous summer, was thirty-five years old at the time, and identified as Black, a native English speaker, and an occasional user of Creole. She also knew French and was taking an advanced course in French literature. She lived in Harlem with her two young daughters. Within months of arriving in New York, Razie began her degree at Bronx Community College, taking two evening classes a week. English 111 was her first writing course and she was eager to make it work. Prof D placed us into writing groups randomly but Razie told me that she thought it was fate we were together, "two old ladies with all of these kids." She was enthusiastic about my scholarship and followed up with me during that semester of my research and then for years afterwards to see if I was moving along with the project. When students signed the IRB protocol, they had the option of being contacted to talk about their experiences after the semester and to choose a research name if they were to appear in the book. Razie contacted me by email the day after signing her IRB form: "My research name is Razie. It's a made-up mix of the names of an author I like, a nurse I know, and my daughters. I love this name. But I don't want a last name; I want to be chill and friendly in the book."

When I read Razie's letter in the first phase of my research, I recalled that unique energy and friendliness. Present at every class session, eager to collect contact information and form study groups, and always sharing drafts and reading material, Razie was very memorable. But later, I reread this letter and acknowledged its place as part of a larger archive of student correspondence, and I contextualized her writing in this evolving story about composition and connection-building. Eighty percent of the students described turned-in, final drafts in the same way Razie did: as "still brewing." They used other phrases; "ongoing," "thinking about it now as I write this," and "continuation of experiencing" were the most common. I think of this pattern as an important definition of what it means to be a lifelong learner. In the reading commons tradition, "learning for learning's sake" is championed as an outcome of a liberal-humanist, literary studies core curriculum. Great books "speak with intimate familiarity about human experiences that we all share," explains a twenty-first-century proponent of these courses (Montás 2021, 7). In these student letters, we see another version of intimacy and another kind of shared familiarity forming. Here human experiences are conjured in writing by nontraditional student authors who are older, working, transfers, multilingual, women of color, parents.

Such reflective, composed experiences are part of the everyday material acts that transform historical events. They are literacy interventions that take place in specific, intimate contexts and in relation to a speaker or writer's identities. And their import can be felt widely. I call on literacy scholar Rhea Estelle Lathan's research as inspiration for this perspective. Lathan's recovery of the "gospel literacy" central to the Civil Rights Movement illuminates intellectual and pedagogical contributions of African Americans. Lathan examines the features of gospel literacies, especially in the Citizenship Schools, and articulates how certain practices (for example, the use of call and response in gospel) contain and conjure "shared memory" and "collective history" (Lathan 2015, 11). Both shared memory and collective history enacted in time and over time are critical to the creation of community and a spiritual and political tradition grounded in freedom. Lathan describes this as a way for the community to bear "witness to their own intellectual value" (2015, 112).

Not aligned with any particular political or social movement, Razie's letter still stands as a statement, a call for readers to respond, or "bear witness," to the intellectual value that reflects the world through writing. Her sample expresses a concern about the relationship between the past and the present, shared by 50 percent of the student letters. Throughout the two semesters, students used the letters to talk about memory. This was especially pronounced in the letters written at the start of the semester. Half of these letters refer to concerns about how memories will interfere with the writing of assignments and the ability, as three letters put it, to "put the past in place," to "write through confusing reminders," or to "get past the way I used to do things."

Memory is an important topic in writing and rhetoric. Discerning forces that influence the making and "uptake" of literacy acts is always challenging, because discourse is informed by social conditions, personal attachments, and "embodied memories" (Bawarshi 2016, 57). Genres, especially official, school-sanctioned ones, will have stable features but are "destabilized" by their "uptake," by how we engage with these genres (Freadman 2012, 560). We tend to pay attention to uptakes in sanctioned school and public discourses and notice their deviations from dominant discourses and their "embodied" memories, something Bawarshi does in his study of the patterns taken up in the US public discourse on Israel-Palestine (2016, 44–58). Yet we might also give attention to repeated patterns of less-formal classroom genres. These genres reveal creative interventions on the dominant genres and ideas about the American academy.

English 111 letters reports are not on geopolitical patterns. Adam and Razie did not collaborate to intervene in political statements, nor did they post their work on social media to garner readers. But their letters codify their embodied memories, identities, and ways of writing into this course and institution and are part of the ever-emergent idea of the university. Their reverberating language affirms their letters as acts of academic diversity, and their memories are brought into relation with each other and with this archive. The letters name the many places where students move through their learning and writing, and they consider how those individual sites, when written about together, are sources of collective learning. They direct us to the middle, where we come to understand what we know and how to share that knowledge with others.

Policymakers and social scientists often debate the possibility of an environmental commons, of whether communities can equitably share land and resources without a top-down hierarchy. Land and resources don't become *shared* land and resources until a community creates that condition, until it is "viewed as such, *by people*, acting together" (Nelson 2015, 4; italics in original). This definition of commons, developed by Dana Nelson in her research on the democratic communities that formed before official American independence, stresses the "bounty of what people can produce together in local community" (2015, 6). Not every classroom is a community, not every classroom produces "bounty." And while these letters were certainly produced together, they were "viewed as such" because I saved the artifacts, read them in context and over time, and noted patterns in language and ideas. Viewing them as such helps us realize the correspondence between reader and writer and between scholar and student. Another way to say this is that research of this kind offers a "reconstructive" reading of these letters.

I conclude this section by adding another response to these letters and introducing the reflective letter I wrote in English 111 to this archive. It, too, can be read as a contribution to the commons. And it may offer readers a place to challenge the idea of the university we are developing here. It is an invitation to write back to this reconstructive read of the academy.

Hi, there,
  So I'll start by saying that this final draft is missing an essence; I circled around the topic rather than land on the core. You asked us to

write about an influential teacher, to use sources, to contextualize the narrative in the time and place of the subject. I went back to my files from fifteen years ago, to my dissertation and the teacher in question, the "subject" and her publications. Still I struggled to place this work with the person I've become since those years. I am the same in some ways: a woman, white, a reader and trying to be a writer, but I am also in mourning. I am sadder now, and also in the middle of this research project, and I don't know when it'll come to something.

REFLECTIVE LETTERS EXTEND AUTHORSHIP

This section centers on one of the letters penned by Sonia Sanchez, an English 111 classmate who challenged everything we did in our composition course. Like the letters by Adam and Razie, Sonia Sanchez's was written at the start of the semester. And like Ashley's freewrite discussed in chapter 3, it draws a parallel between commuting to school and communicating in writing. Sonia was not her real first name; it was the name she chose to accompany her last name, Sanchez. She had read a poem written by Sonia Sanchez in high school and was interested in the Black Arts Movement. She wrote poetry on her own but told me at the start of the semester that she didn't want anyone to think she was "flighty." Sanchez spent a good deal of time with Adam, as they were in several classes together and walked to the library after class each week.

Twenty years old at the time of this research, Sonia Sanchez identified as Dominican American and "definitely single." She split her time between Brooklyn and the Bronx, and lived with family members who spoke both Spanish and English at home. She hoped to major in psychology and English while keeping a new job, as assistant to the bookkeeper at a doctor's office, learning how to drive, and attending weekly meetings with a speech therapist. Sanchez said she had probably had dyslexia since elementary school but did not seek treatment until college. After one semester at a community college, she left school to take a job at the Catholic high school she attended. This was Sanchez's first time registered as a full-time undergraduate; she was taking five courses and working eighteen hours a week.

Months after the semester ended, Sanchez told me she was double-majoring and, though she was not "yet a great student," aimed to get "As" in her Professional Writing courses. "I don't have time for extraneousness," she would often say aloud to no one in particular, but within earshot of the instructor. Students liked Sanchez because she would say what lots of us were thinking. Prof D seemed to appreciate her candor.

"Does this writing count towards our grade?"; "How long should this essay be?"; and "Why are we doing this, again?" were Sanchez's first questions about any activity we did in class.

The professor of our course spent a lot of time, more than any teacher I've known, explaining the purposes of assignments and the skills that could be gained from class activities. Sanchez liked Prof D for that and told me this instructor was the best professor she ever had, "challenging" but "fair." Still, Sanchez retained a sense of suspicion about informal writing throughout the semester. She said her formal, graded assignments should "just speak for themselves." In the case of this first reflective letter, Sanchez had expressed confidence in her final product, describing it as "quality work, clear writing, specific details given." She wonders about the benefits of returning to what is done and done well. And she questions the claim made by many scholars that "self-monitoring" aids in learning and knowledge (Yancey 2016, 7). Here is her letter:

> Dear Reader:
>   Wait. For real, is this a letter that starts us over? Interesting. I know the essay is finished and getting graded. Mine is good, clear writing, specific details given. But look, we're kind of starting it again now with this letter. We are repeating, over and over, the same thing a little differently. Wondering how to start this letter. And who writes letters anyway? If we're writing then we are going to end up adding, changing, and doing more than expected or required. We need different kinds of time. We are going **beyond** and **beginning again**.
>
>   Bye,
>   Sanchez

We see how rhetorical scholar Sanchez raises doubt about the good reflective writing can do for self or society. In this way, her correspondence connects to the point made by rhetorical scholar Casey Boyle. Boyle sees reflective activities generating "bad habits" for students. Reflection is an epistemology that favors two-dimensionality; it separates self from objects and asserts a need to be "above all others" (Boyle 2016, 544). Conjuring research in posthumanism and object-oriented rhetoric, Boyle describes process genres like the reflective letter as reifying a Western, Enlightenment idea of individualism. Reflection focuses on the human subject as outside of the network of systems embedding it. But we are never not in a relationship with technologies, species, and human and nonhuman actors (Boyle 2016, 540). In turn, Boyle suggests that writing courses focus on multiple forms of practice and not on process activities. Practice requires repetition. And in the repetition something different evolves, something "ongoing" and "serial." The "events of practice overlap and contribute new versions of what might otherwise be seen as the same" (Boyle 2018, 34).

Sanchez's sample opens with a similarly astute critique of reflection. This critique happens *because* she is actually writing a letter, and considering her place in this genre. That is one of the central paradoxes and potentials of this practice as I see it. "Wait. For real," she begins. These are colloquial expressions that alert the reader to read on, to find what matters next. They put pressure on the interlocutor to place observation on the making of this task, as it happens. As Boyle describes practice—"repeating . . . the same thing a little differently"—Sanchez describes her reflective letter. In this practice comes a persuasive claim and a theory. The sample makes an argument about what it takes materially to revise "different kinds of time." And the letter situates this claim—the need to give students more time—as a theory and ethics of the commons. It counts as knowledge the ongoing act of change and transformation, of going "beyond" the expectations of others and integrating new versions of the self, in concert with others, into knowledge-making.

"And who writes letters anyway?" Sanchez wonders. This is a question any contemporary writer or teacher might ask. Why not teach a different genre for building a commons, especially in this digital, global, and inequitable world? Collaborative, digital projects are often described as genres that matter to today's learner. These are common to personal and professional discourse, and teaching them may also help students resist the humanist vision of a solitary subject. James Rushing Daniel sees collaborative writing activities, especially genres like the public-facing political statement, as important for composition studies today. These activities and genres have "confrontational capacities" and can challenge the "logics of neoliberalism" and "support anticapitalist change" (Daniel 2022, 40). Recognized by Daniel is the "thorny contradiction that plagues" pedagogy on these discourses. While we may teach collaborative digital media forms so that students make bonds outside of the marketplace, we generate and disseminate this writing on platforms built to mine our data and profit from our information and literacy (Daniel 2022, 146). There is no getting around the contradiction. But I suggest that the reflective letter offers a unique confrontation with it. Sanchez described reflective letters as a process of "beginning again," of writing being an act of always sitting between places, ideas, persons, and positions. The letter, as a form of correspondence, helped articulate this view. It is an example of how to not just represent diversity but engage diverse authors.

The letters by Sanchez and others remind readers to reach beyond reform and encounter the lived-in engagement with course material and the act of writing itself. The idea that curricular reforms do not alone alter higher education is something we learn from the work of Lorgia García Peña. *Community As Rebellion: A Syllabus for Surviving Academia as a Woman of Color*, García Peña's manifesto about belonging, diversity, and liberation pedagogy, began as a "letter to my students" (2022, xiv). At one point, that genre was the right tool to express, document, and record frustration over being silenced at an academic conference. She used the letter to conjure a counterconference, where scholars and students, mostly women of color, collaborated and shared ideas. They found "*another* way of imagining the academy" (García Peña 2022, xiv, xv).

Like the Latinx Student Alliance letter, García Peña lists goals for fighting the status quo and recognizing the contributions of anti-racist, decolonial scholars. These include, first, understanding the "legacy" of the work in ethnic studies and among BIPOC; second, forcing the university to adopt programs and practices that do more than talk about inclusion; and third, recognizing faculty of color labor—mentoring and service, for example—that goes beyond research. But unless all of these goals are practiced and are part of the everyday activity of the academy, the "project of 'diversity and inclusion'" must be called a failure (García Peña 2022, 97).

The project of diversity and inclusion as represented in the Lehman College English department has only partially succeeded. We are not yet committed to investing in student practices as diverse, inclusive knowledge-making and authorship. As a way to conclude this chapter, I want to bring student practices back into this project on authorship to see how reading reflective letters centers students in the project of diversity, inclusion, and creating a commons.

REFLECTIVE LETTERS AND CLOSE, COMMUTIVE READING

On October 24 and December 5 of my fall semester in English 111, students were once again prompted to "recount the steps taken to write and complete" an assignment. This time, the assignment focused on close reading. The topic for these two essays was the role of technology in higher education. That subject was unique to our section of English 111. But every Lehman College English 111 class required an argumentative essay built from published sources to make a "claim" from "close textual reading." For weeks, we read essays about technology, learning, identity, and shifts in higher education published in scholarly journals, our course collection, and popular media.[11] Of the forty-five collected over the fall 2012 term, I've chosen four samples from my collection:

1. Can we **return** to the reading? I need to deal with Carr's references. We went through the Carr essay very closely when we broke down arguments like we did with Tan and Nguyen and Barry's piece. Carr read a lot, skims a bunch. Look at his references. I have not read the references (like Taylor, Nietzsche) and I am thinking we could divide up these amongst us, get a list of deep reading going, then write a collective response? This way we'd read closely with a wide **reach**, so as to share what we found out.

2. We did a good job connecting this essay with Tan and Barry and others. I am **reconsidering** the Carr and Richtel essays and feel like I'm working through both and putting them really together, especially what Carr argues in his introduction with the repetition of the verb "feel" I think four times.

3. Need to get into what I'm saying about Tan's essay and Englishes. There's so much more to say about what she talks about, I love it. But it's not complete in terms of what we know is possible with being multilingual, though we didn't write about that at length. We could do that work. Then **come back** to this essay.

4. The essay is okay but I did not cover all of the Carr essay, just quoting from his opening and **closely reading** how we talked about "concentration" in attention. If I were to see these other letters, I'd reconsider where to go with this for next time.

The samples were written after we completed essays that asked us to closely read published material. This reading material was to serve as evidence to make the claim of the essay. Yet in 80 percent of the letters, students use the present and future tense. It's as if this writing was still in process and their reading ongoing, happening in close proximity to these reflective letters. The letters say very little about the arguments of their final essays or the assigned reading, and quite a bit about the unfinished work of interpretation. Five letters mention the term "argument," three use "evidence" and "textual," and three discuss the "proof" used in the formal essays. But thirty letters give some additional readings of essays, especially Amy Tan's "Mother Tongue" and Nicholas Carr's "Is Google Making Us Stupid?" Twenty reference particular passages or closely read footnotes or references from the published texts. Twenty-three describe how they might put the parts of their essays "really together." Twenty-six letters include some questions about how to "reconsider" past readings for the needs of the moment and those to come.

The prompt directed students to recount the steps taken to compose and complete argumentative essays based on close reading of textual evidence. Students respond with a set of new close readings, connecting again to the texts and to background knowledge gained or lacking from those previous encounters. The letters collect traces of text, information, and knowledge that didn't come through in close readings, and then return to those traces as the sources of new readings. And while the prompt asked for individual responses and the letters were directed to a single reader, 75 percent of the letters move from the pronoun "I" to the pronoun "we." The letters also read into the background of the authors. Students dissect the reading habits of published authors and compare them with their own. Sample one speaks of Nicholas Carr and his extensive experience as a professional critic. The letter makes us turn back to Carr to see him as an author who "references." This is different from an author who reads closely and with "attention." Sample three connects to the assigned Amy Tan essay but sees her thinking about multilingualism as "incomplete." This letter was finished at the end of the term, and the writer was supposed to assess her last assignment. Instead, she offers a lesson plan for future student authors. This writer asks her reader to consider how a close reading of Tan's essay might reveal different insights if were read alongside essays about multilingualism written by students.

Similarly, sample one repurposes the directive to close read by reframing attention to Carr's "surface" reading, or his multiple textual layering. Literary critics compare "symptomatic reading" with "surface reading." The former is akin to close reading. Close reading, as I. A. Richards and the other architects of Harvard's postwar polemic explained, was the central methodology of the generally educated American, the critical tool of a "free society." Close reading focuses on depth, on the belief that textual truths are usually "present but invisible" and must be deciphered (Best and Marcus 2009, 4). Surface reading, on the other hand, focuses on "materiality" or what forms for readers as their immediate reaction; critics see this as a liberation from the regimen of close reading (Best and Marcus 2009, 9). In the reflective letters, students practice neither approach. We might think here of Eve Kosofsky Sedgwick's reparative reading strategy, which encouraged a paranoid-free kind of "enabling" or surprise-oriented approach to texts (Sedgwick 1997, 146). Sedgwick's reparative reading strategy made the convincing case that we learn to interpret texts for the "many ways selves and communities succeed in extracting sustenance" from cultural material (150). There is sustenance in these student letters, enough to form an alliance with Sedgwick's queer-oriented intervention in methodology. However, I see the letters as doing something else: reversing the usual power differential in approaches to reading.

We recall Carr's contribution to the reading commons, described in chapter 2. In his award-winning essay "Is Google Making Us Stupid," and in the book that followed, Carr echoed a familiar complaint about American readers: they lack deep concentration. In these letters, students write back to Carr, to a theory of authorship, and to a reading commons idea of the university. They insert their own references into this conversation about reading and concentration. In this way they not only read deeply but, to quote the LSA letter, as a "reflection of the world." The reflective texts also embed students' experience into the interpretive process, offering a "reparative" reading of the close reading assignment and reinventing it.

Reflective letters offer an alternative to close reading that is also "commutive." A commutive engagement with texts resonates with a theory developed by poet and teacher Juliana Spahr, whose approach is less concerned with "deciphering" literature and more attuned to "what sorts of communities works encourage" (Spahr 2001, 5). The poetry and novels studied in her 2001 book *Everybody's Autonomy* are drawn from diverse areas of the nation and world and also represent particular, recognizable interests. However, Spahr sees her reading theory as a widely applicable methodology, a "formal" approach to creating ties among people and ideas through close reading and collective responses to reading (Spahr 2001, 5). Most of her evidence of collective response comes from her classroom. For example, Spahr traces the "emphatic relation" that teaching Gertrude Stein offers multilinguals. How students connect to Stein matters more than whether they comprehend "the meaning" of the literature, Spahr writes, because, over time, they link to the language possibilities of her work (Spahr 2001, 43). Language possibilities become visible through representation. Spahr teaches authors traditionally ignored in general education classes. When readers confront their limitations and conflicts with authors and texts, these possibilities extend. Spahr describes this experience teaching Hawai'ian poet Grace Molisa's work. Molisa's poems about small islands and global conditions perform tensions that are always present in reading. The tensions between being rooted in a place—in this case, a postcolonial state—and seeking autonomy through writing—are critical to literacy's connective work in the world (Spahr 2001, 9).

A commutive approach is a mobile approach; the connection a reader makes between text and self and between text and community happens somewhere in the middle of close and surface reads. Lived-in letters, like those we did in English 111, concretize this connection and then continue it. These letters are "commutive" because they take this relationship beyond the local situation, offering a way to understand the navigation that happens as readers meet texts, and what happens surrounding that meeting. In the previous chapter we examined scholarship focused on the "mobility condition" of our world. Educators concerned with the "unsteady state" of students and society see writing as a way to seek and create "an alternative foundation" (Horner et al. 2021, 7). Lived-in letters provide a temporary foundation for students and the academy, connecting lifeworlds with our social and intellectual experiences. For Charlemae Hill Rollins and Holland D. Roberts, letter writing was one way to ensure that intercultural and experience-based curricula were dynamic and spoke to the complexities of literacy and culture.

Many professors turn reflective letters into content for the course, as Rollins and Roberts did. Doing this helps students notice the resonances among language and phrasing, connecting their thinking to the thinking of experts. But this content can move past the classroom, too. I have turned to this content as material for understanding the academy. Content is "something contained." It is also the "subject matter or symbolic significance of something" and a state of "peaceful satisfaction."[12] In other words, content is an affect and an abstraction, and it is something actual. Content includes reading assignments, writing prompts, final essays, and assessments. And it is frustrations, unfinished material, and ideas surrounding texts left adrift, hovering around the kitchen table or in memories.

Reflective letters are said to provide information for teachers or researchers about the skills and knowledge that have been captured for export or transfer. In the case of this archive, they provide a prompt for the student to turn unfinished work into new writing. The samples we see here were written at the end of the semester but realize the work that happens in the middle, between reading encounter and textual meaning. Though both students finished the required reading, their work is "not complete." In the act of corresponding about their close reading, they direct the reader to what is not covered in the mastery of critical texts. For example, sample three suggests that we need more research on meaning-making by multilingual readers. Sample four makes the case, in direct opposition to the argument in *Academically Adrift*, that concentration and attention are not always the outcome of spending hours in solitary, direct engagement with texts.

In finding patterns in the letters, I need to address what Asao B. Inoue and Tyler Richmond name as a "common set of rhetorical tropes" that form around student groups, especially minoritized students (Inoue and Richmond 2016, 130). Inoue's 2015 book *Antiracist Writing Assessment*

Ecologies provides insight into how reflective letters work to illuminate or reify parts of our social and intellectual lives. He draws on Pierre Bourdieu's notion of "habitus" to conjure the relationship between writing and the structures of social interactions that organize history and society (Inoue 2015, 42). Race is one socially constructed organizing principle in the ecology of education. To work towards an anti-racist pedagogy, curricula, or assessment approach, we need to think about the various, complex, intersecting structures, including race, that are part of teaching and learning. I've tried to attend to the features of individual letters and to how they might affect other social interactions. In doing so, I attempt to read these letters as correspondences that reflect the world and reconstruct it. Habitus is a through line in reflective letters, though students use synonyms: world, home, culture, society, self, and other. The material of academically emergent knowledge is made in the material and existential conditions of interruptions, parts, and beginning again.

Literary critic John Guillory also adopts the word *habitus* to unpack what curricular debates say about our understanding of "cultural capital," or what counts as knowledge (1993). Guillory offers important insight into the academy's obsession with canons. That obsession takes attention away from the variety of inventive, collective forms of common learning and leads him to claim that general education and the whole "experiment" of mass secondary education "remains to be imagined" (Guillory 2006, 45). Guillory's more recent accounting of the academy's habitus is equally bleak. He sees dire realities to come, with shrinking interest in literary studies and no standards or set modalities for writing or reading cultural criticism (Guillory 2022). A clear-eyed take on shifts in the creation and professionalization of culture and criticism is essential, to be sure. But we need not be so pessimistic, or even imaginative, to invigorate our understanding of cultural capital and notice how student genres are vitalizing an intellectual commons. Reflective letters are these genres, creating the content of an idea of the university as a public commons. They realize the habitus of individual students who are nontraditional and also inventing their relationship to the academy.

We have some examples of pedagogy and practice that yields this kind of content. One comes from Felicia Rose Chavez's 2021 book *The Anti-Racist Writing Workshop*. Like Rollins's *We Build Together* or Burrows's *They All Want to Write*, Chavez's targeted audience for her book about the creative writing workshop is anyone interested in liberatory pedagogy. The pedagogy described here, however, belongs at the center of composition courses. Chavez sets out to remake the dynamics in the traditional creative writing workshop and uses freewriting as one approach that can reconfigure power in the classroom. She sees "daily freewriting exercises" and other informal correspondences as "risking voice" and promoting "wandering" so that students, especially students of color, can "own their own terms" and, after repeated practice and repetition, gain a "critical vocabulary of craft" and a "shared vocabulary" (Chavez 2021, 34, 5). Our classrooms can be places where students "wrest" writing free from historic boundaries. Students need to make their own traditions in the company of other forms of knowledge and to extend that tradition to other students and to the academy (Chavez 2021, 35).

Chavez sees a shared vocabulary as essential to achieving general writing goals, like "voice, imagery, characterization, and arrangement" (2021, 34). The Stanford Language Arts Investigation called freewriting contact composition because it engaged with "background knowledge" that gets made and "enlarged" by others; reflective letters move this knowledge into the commons. If we read it as "cultural material" of academia, it contributes to an ever-diverse, public commons. To write with students and see this writing as forming culture is to take an activist view of authorship. When students freewrite and reflect often, alongside each other, and when this work is read, we move past the culture of "crisis in creative writing" or crisis in the humanities and into another way of making "American culture" (Chavez 2021, 11). Informal writing recognizes "spoken" and "felt" language and has the potential to redistribute "power equitably among participants and instructors" and to generate collective, "democratic learning spaces" (Chavez 2021, 7, 8).

Collective power does not look like one thing. It can come in many forms, including assignment prompts made in public and composed in private. Sharon Marshall makes this point in a 2009 essay about the importance of informal composing done in classrooms. Private freewriting will not always contribute to a core curriculum or represent shifts in a canon. Yet it produces real content, and this material matters precisely because it is not co-opted by the systems that surround and seep into everything we do. Marshall grounds her thinking in Nichiren Buddhism, in her "negative experiences" as a Black woman in a predominately white school, and in response to "a love of reading and writing, a disdain for traditional schooling, and a fear of racially motivated exclusion" (Marshall 2009, 9). Private in-class writing is an "individual act performed in public," of being "in but not of" the institution (Marshall 2009, 21; Harney and Moten 2013, 12). In *The Undercommons,* Harney and Moten see the "path of the subversive intellectual in the modern university" as an activity embedded in the existing social structures but not concerned with "worry" or "reform" (12). For Marshall, private writing does not get made outside these systems and structures of power. But neither does it serve the conforming function of many pedagogies and programs. Unlike most pedagogies and curricula, it is content that creates an "environment" and the "dual, even paradoxical" world-making work of being in but not of the self who seeks the other, not in harmony always but in "awareness" (2009, 8).

"Awareness," for Marshall, describes the paradoxical, contradictory work of classrooms, with its private writing and public-facing literacies. Alvina Treut Burrows chooses "atmosphere" and "power." Both call for a space in academia for what Chavez names "creative concentration" (Chavez 2021, 11). One way to create this space is to diversify content. Another is to assign writing that accompanies reading and to see the writers as engaged in a collective project to expand authorship. The SLAI researchers put it this way: educators have to be "accountable" to emerging and "expanding forms of human experience." To do that, they will need to make lived-in composition practices a social and cultural matter (Kaulfers and Roberts 1937, 4). Reflective letters enable teachers, scholars, administrators, and students to be part of a "beginning again" of the academy. They attend to the lived compositions and correspondences of students as authoring the idea of the university. They are the "reflection of the world" in practice.

CODA: ON INFLUENCE

Some years after I conducted the research for this book, I was gathering scholarship about reflection and reflective genres. And I learned of a piece about the topic written by Pat Belanoff. Her 2001 "Silence: Reflection, Literacy, Learning and Teaching" traces the origins of reflection as an epistemology and ontology. "Silence" shows how reflection works as a genre, in and across multiple cultural materials, from medieval literature to pedagogies of the contemporary classroom.

This essay asks how reflection becomes discourse. Belanoff considers the relationship between intellectual abstraction and material culture and the role of reflection in embodying that relationship. When we reflect, she muses, we must attend to the object of reflection and also stray from it, and from dominant structures of knowing. For instance, Belanoff offers an extended close reading of what Inoue might call the "ecologies" found in a burial stone. The medieval stone carving she chooses to analyze is of an animal and human face layered on top of another. Belanoff calls such "texts" reflective because they resist endings and beginnings, are human and constructed, and defy any single interpretation or observation. From here, Belanoff argues that reflective genres represent, rehearse, and return to places and times that seem invisible but can be conjured through collective mediation on the material world. She concludes that reflection works at the "interlace" of literacy. Reflective letters allow us directed "detours," to be present in the "web of interconnectedness of saying and doing" (Belanoff 2001, 417, 414).

Pat Belanoff was the subject of my first essay written as a student-researcher in English 111. I wrote about her for that assignment and again in the opening reflective letter assigned. That letter is transcribed in this chapter. It did not follow the prompt; it was not about the steps I took to compose the final assignment. The English 111 assignment had asked for an essay on an "influential teacher." My reflective letter talks about my trouble writing about that influence. It took a detour. And that detour brought us here, to reflection as a form of reconstructing the academy.

The letter was hard to write and to read again. It was even harder to make public here. I wrote it at a certain time, when I was in a raw place. Maybe it will be read with some objective distance. Maybe it will be read as evidence that letters lead to bad habits in academia. I can't predict the reader response. But I know it was part of the shifts needed to begin again in academia after the pandemic, to reconsider a "middle" connection between the academy and the world we live in now. A temporal, spatial, and interpretive texture surround that relationship. The reflective letters commute it; I can articulate the feeling of loss from that time and the power in composing that feeling with others. As a letter, that feeling and those relationships became part of something outside of myself. We are all bound in that literacy interlace.

In English 111 we wrote our letters to our professors, other students, administrators, and our former and emerging selves. But we also wrote these letters to "you": we who look to the intimate space of classroom correspondence to reconstruct the world society of writers.

Conclusion

AN IDEA MADE IN THE PRACTICES OF THE PUBLIC

I began this book at the start of a global pandemic. It will likely be read as we continue to work through the wreckage of that crisis. There was much to do before the Covid-19 outbreak and there's more to do now as we build a different university for a different world. And there's frustrating delay and some derailing in our efforts to bring about change: secure fair labor practices, equitable admission procedures, updated facilities, credit allocation for working students, campus childcare centers, and necessary funding for writing programs. This is only a partial list of problems facing the public academy and my particular corner of it, writing studies. Given the challenges ahead, it's fair to ask, as I often did over these last years, why, given this state of the world and public education, focus on forgotten file cabinets, with a few hundred freewrites and letters written by college composition students and teachers? And why insist that these practices can propel a new *idea* of the university?

I imagine these questions did not plague Cardinal Newman when he penned *The Idea of a University* two centuries ago. Newman wrote *The Idea of a University* to honor the Catholic University in Dublin, bestowing the institution with universal beauty and truth, and the liberal arts with the essence of transcendence. I wrote *The Composition Commons* to honor the students and faculty of CUNY and the many institutions like it, detailing how everyday literacy encounters have profound power. How best to honor these encounters is something I grappled with in this project and something many of us who study, teach, and advocate in public and nonprestigious colleges and universities grapple with every day. Throughout these pages, I've tried to confront my own limitations and those of my profession. We humanists have a tendency to traffic in grandiosity and pathos when attached to certain texts and theories just as we compositionists can put too much faith in critical pedagogy and rhetorical reasoning in pursuit of creative, constructive literacy and learning. My research attempted to acknowledge where the actual and aspirational connect and clash, when rendering a world society of writers

https://doi.org/10.7330/9781646425433.c005

requires particularized attention to politics and power. And my reading of student texts and programs attempts to position these in the material conditions of time and place and, also as critical interventions in the formation of intellectual history.

But still, this book is about a big idea and its manifestation in small practices. When we commit to bringing the grand and granular together, when we insist that they coexist and that this cohabitation creates culture, we risk sliding into nostalgia or fantasy. But risk is something that student writers take all the time, when they engage in contact-oriented, reconstructive practices. So by way of conclusion, then, I risk making the case for composition as an idea and a course of action that can build a new kind of academic commons.

FROM THE LIBERAL ARTS TO LIBERATORY PRACTICES

The crisis and reform period that followed World War II offered an opportunity to remake the academy in the practices of the public. That was the hope of the Stanford Language Arts Investigation. Had educators and policymakers invested in this idea, maybe we'd have a different kind of university today. Instead they discredited the experiment, citing problems with its research and pedagogy but actually refusing its radically inclusive approach to knowledge.

This moment offers another opportunity, a chance to rekindle a public academic commons. But we'll need to forge a different path than the one taken by many contemporary thinkers. For example, in two new academic manifestos, Roosevelt Montás's *Rescuing Socrates* and Arnold Weinstein's *The Lives of Literature*, we learn how the classical education of old will rescue us anew. Once and forever, the "institution of reading" will invigorate the university and democracy (Weinstein, 2021, 330). During the pandemic, we're told, the reading idea of the university served as salve for a suffering student body. Literature released us from us from isolation and gave students, "imprisoned in their family homes," a place to go for "social immersion" (75).

This is a liberation ideology built on a liberal arts tradition made for and by elites. For Montás, Columbia's historic common core curriculum, with its great books courses required of every undergraduate, enables "the condition of human freedom and self-determination" (2021, 2). There is no such requirement at Brown, where Weinstein teaches. Nevertheless the great books are what creates a "fellowship of spirits"; they are "as democratic as air itself" (Weinstein 2021, 330, 136).

To be sure, reading can be revelatory. Montás's own experience proves that books change lives. He describes arriving in the United States from the Dominican Republic with limited English-language skills and little money and then enrolling at Columbia University through the New York State Higher Education Opportunity Program (HEOP). There, he found literature. His particular journey is moving. But it is of limited value when it serves as the moral of a century-old story about the liberal arts: great books can heal the self and "subvert the hierarchies" of social life (12).

Even like-minded humanists can't help but raise an eyebrow at this full-throated faith in literature to heal us or be the best weapon to fight injustice. The very notion that democracy "hinges" on the fate of liberal education is not only out of touch, it's delusional, writes Louis Menand (2021), in his scathing review of *Rescuing Socrates* and *The Lives of Literature*. A chorus has erupted to second this critique. It seems like every week another article comes out to analyze how literary studies lost its pride of place as the cultural epicenter of democratic values and human ingenuity. Big tech is where the real imaginative action is now, writes Nathan Heller in his February 2023 piece for the *New Yorker*. Heller's report bids goodbye to the stuffy seminar room of literature majors to take readers on a tour of airy new cathedrals of creativity rising up on campuses. In these gleaming glass towers, brilliant students don't just study engineering or robotics in labs and classrooms but innovate in "maker-spaces."

This sounds like a promotional event for STEM and a last will and testament for the humanities and English departments. But as the essay comes to an end, it is to the power of words where Heller goes. In his interviews with undergraduates about their college experience, Heller recounts their commitment to, of all things, writing. One student describes loving to read because she wants to write. Her testimony echoes a growing trend in higher education: while enrollments in literature courses are down, interest in writing courses are up.[1]

Heller might have looked at some of these courses thriving on campuses not often highlighted in the *New Yorker*. Yet Heller's eulogy for English ends where many writing courses begin: in possibility, in present realities, in the potential to construct something new with craft and interpersonal connection. There are many sites of innovation in the academy. But the public, composition classroom has been sorely overlooked. Montás and other literary critics are right to argue that "great books" programs can be invigorated, so they belong to everyone. That does not mean they generate belonging *for* everyone. As I've been suggesting throughout this book, if, as Weinstein argues, a "fellowship of spirits" is a goal of education, we need to find that fellowship in the places and practices where students find connection and collectives without the architecture of "social immersion," like dorms, that structure intellectual camaraderie. Writing is that practice and the public academy is that space.

But our most-cited chroniclers of the university don't go there.[2] The general population and a good portion of the academy still see writing courses as service classes. They are not where we germinate the sense of collective knowledge that matters to culture. In *The Marketplace of Ideas*, Louis Menand's important history of higher education, composition gets one mention: in a footnote. "Expository Writing," Menand acknowledges, is almost universally required for undergraduates. But it has not earned a spot in the story about America's "marketplace of ideas." That's because the writing course doesn't inspire epistemological controversy and encourage change. General education, on the other hand, is where colleges "actually think about the outcomes of the experience they provide" (2010, 32). Writing is more like the "once common . . . swimming test": necessary to survive but not to thrive (25).

I cite this not to rehearse old grievances. It hardly counts as breaking news to report esteemed scholars caught in the act of overlooking composition.[3] While there will always be myopic manifestos about the academy there will always be those who show us another way, as writing scholars have done for decades.[4] Recently, literary critics have joined compositionists in chronicling classroom activity as an engine of culture and intellectual history. Kathleen Fitzpatrick provides evidence from her digital humanities teaching to offer fresh and "generous" approaches to learning about cultures and literacies alive in today's America. Subjects focused on literature, writing, history, the arts, and interpretation give us a chance to read "together" and do the "public work" of collective knowledge-making.

Reading together is one way the academy can focus on a social good that is not privatized or market-driven but addresses experimentation and community. The humanities in this model uses tools of the present to look closely at texts of the past. Here, "careful study and analysis of cultures and their many modes of thought and representation" offer opportunities for people to engage with and make ethical contributions to the world (Fitzpatrick 2019, 20). Fitzpatrick's work connects with many projects taking a public good approach to a diverse, global, digital-era academy. My own university has engaged in such social-justice humanities endeavors. As part of the Transformative Learning in the Humanities (TLH) Mellon grant, my colleagues and I experiment with and challenge our approaches to teaching and confront staid beliefs about higher learning. We collaborate across areas and levels, generating public-facing programs for local and wider audiences. Our purpose is to innovate classrooms and engage students where they are now. We also want to rethink the role of a liberal arts and literacy education for a more equitable future.[5]

These innovations are tied to a desire for humanists to engage with "activist presentism" so that the liberal arts can be part of a movement to diversify and update higher education. This kind of presentism does not ignore history. Rather it engages in texts of the past to "begin to allow our fields more appropriately to represent the voices and experiences of the past and the present that have remained marginalized or entirely unheard" (Spratt and Draxler 2019). Interest in reading strategies that are "postcritical" is part of an effort to take a generative and communal approach to textual study. Rita Felski's *The Limits of Critique* defines close and "suspicious" interpretive reading as essentializing, calling on academics to begin "disinvesting" from these approaches. Doing so enables literary studies to embrace more "affective styles and modes of argument" (2015, 3).

One manifestation of this style and mode comes from Rachel Sagner Buurma and Laura Heffernan's *The Teaching Archive*. To reclaim literary studies as relevant in the twenty-first century and extricate it from its Eurocentric, elitist past, the pair suggest that scholars turn their attention to history made in the "the teaching archive." In studying artifacts produced in the classrooms of such literary giants as T. S. Eliot, a new past emerges, more inclusive and less limiting. It's a past "we need now more than ever" in light of the defunding crisis of higher education and attacks on the non-STEM courses (Buurma and Heffernan 2020, 213).

We should continue to recover marginalized cultures and histories and see how they reorient history. And it is a good thing to embrace literary studies as a vibrant subject for enlarging our understanding of data, knowledge, and culture. But the composition commons I forward here is not about adding to or reinventing the reading commons. It is about its reconstruction.

Reconstructing the academy was one of the central purposes of the Stanford Language Arts Investigation. Their work in composition found that shared knowledge and common experience spill out of informal writing activities invented "at the beginning" of one's connection to academia. That is because these genres form a contact point between individual background knowledge and a collective sense of belonging, so that new content forms in a course and for the academy.

The SLAI did not attach this finding to a discipline or paradigm. They were not humanists or compositionists. Indeed, these teacher-researchers were suspicious of zealous reforms, suspecting they were not up to the painstakingly person-to-person task of cultivating material in the literacies of the "new" American students. Louise Noyes, Alvina Burrows, Charlemae Rollins, Holland D. Roberts, Walter Kaulfers, and the other SLAI participants were wary of both liberal-humanist and progressive general education agendas. They predicted, quite rightly, that these models would fail to notice the "power" of informal practices authored by students attending nonprestige institutions. So, in defiance of the dominant approaches to the commons, these 1930s educators offered a third idea of the university.

Thinking of the composition commons as a third idea of the university resonates with critical posthumanist theorists, digital rhetors, and pedagogues, like N. Katherine Hayles, who believe in a humanities that is in search of new forms of being. Relying on texts and our interpretation of them will not yield the collective, creative connections we desire and need today. Instead of claiming culture and knowledge as constructed by the social, or seeking ways of escape from these forces, Hayles proposes a "third alternative" for the humanities, one that recognizes the challenges and paradoxes of thinking through, and in, crisis. She asks that we embrace our cultural constraints, acting "in dynamic conjunction with metaphoric language," and that we "articulate the rich possibilities of distributed cognitive systems that include human and nonhuman actors" (Hayles 2001, 158).

Composition courses provide an opportunity for embracing constraints, accessing language, and engaging with possibilities. This view of the commons requires that writing courses be moved from footnote to the core in our story of innovation in the American academy. And it means that the composition course should be supported and funded as central to a new kind of general education, one that aims to discover and encourage literacy practices created by student writers attending public institutions. They are not the only builders of the academic commons. But they are significant composers and we need to invest in their places and practices. That means centering the composition course in the American academy.

THE CASE FOR COMPOSITION AS THE
CORE OF COMMONS LEARNINGS

I make the claim for composition with some caveats. There is no such thing as the "college composition course." First-year writing, or English 111, or whatever we name it, is different at every institution, and different sections taught at the same institution can vary widely. And the concerns about composition are also diffuse. They depend on the local circumstances of particular colleges and universities.[6] One problem with first-year writing, especially pronounced at large, public, nonprestigious universities like my own, is how composition programs perpetuate unjust labor practices among teachers. At CUNY, scholars and students have been fighting against austerity measures that hurt teachers and students and reify racist and classist courses.[7] Doing so is necessary; we cannot advocate for students, scholarship, and education justice without arguing for material changes to the academy, especially in funding for public colleges and universities.

But change has come slowly or not at all. That is why some suggest we get out of the fight altogether by abolishing the compulsory composition course and divesting from student writing as an object of scholarly study. That was the political position Sharon Crowley took in the 1990s, when she detailed how the course perpetuates inequalities. Sidney I. Dobrin takes a more intellectual stance against composition. He writes that an "attachment to students rather than to theory or research" relegates writing to the margins of academia, to "nothing more than an academic, administrative entity permitted the space of FYC and little more" (2011, 20–21). Dobrin cautions against the kind of research I've done here, about genres germinated in the first-year composition course. This course, he finds, lacks epistemological heft and, in turn, ideological import. Any hope of "real emancipatory work" in the academy must be "disassociated from the classroom" (2011, 13).

I agree with Dobrin that some writing programs peddle in myths of the past and some scholars are tied to short-term serviceable goals. However, where we differ is in a definition of "real emancipatory work." I believe that it is not the time to create distance from student writing or from a class devoted to student writers. Not when nontraditional students are becoming the academic majority in America, writing new ideas of, and in, a changing university. Emancipatory work can be messy, confrontational, and without furnished theory. But it exists, found in unfinished, emergent compositions of student authors.

The composition course has its own problems with its own historical baggage. Yet it is unique in the academy, because it is not a course rooted in *representing* an idea of a university. Rather it is a course that drafts ideas about, and in, the tense spaces of social and intellectual life. The composition class as I am thinking about it here is engaged with questions concerning "crisis ordinariness," Lauren Berlant's phrase for the "process" of social life that "unfolds" in everyday life (2009, 10). I came across Berlant's most recent meditations on crisis ordinariness, crafted during the pandemic and published posthumously, as I finished this project. *On the Inconvenience of Other People* turns to the same concept I highlight here, "the commons," to navigate the changes in our social world and in the "fractious middle of life" (Berlant 2022, x). In addition to the stunning title of this book, which performs the struggle of believing in and building connections with others, *On the Inconvenience of Other People* details a commons tradition in American poetry, where words and things, intimacy and distance coexist, often in an "uncoordinated" balance (2022, 97).

I have found poetics and coexistence in another American tradition: the composition classroom. There is a living, learning archive of contact and connection found in this commons if we redefine the general skills course differently and think about first-year writing beyond the usual formations: as a service for or "gateway" to real knowledge-making. Many of the composition courses we have now already teach important skills: critical thinking, reasoning, argument, and clarity in writing. And writing classes are not the only places where we can take a rhetorically nuanced position on communication, learning, and knowledge. We don't need to adjudicate the point that every situation, audience, genre, and medium will require a different kind of writing. What we do need is a course that can notice the tensions in trying to write and reach out to others in a shifting commons atmosphere.

Research in classroom archives leaves me encouraged by the prospects of composition as a course that enacts practices of the commons. In attending to informal compositions, we see how the college composition course can be the area of the academy devoted to discovering what happens when we write together and observe the epistemological and social contributions of these forms of belonging. Informal genres of the commons let us see what *could* happen in a writing class: the creation of a living archive of cultural material that represents but also requires rigorous attention to the moment when one expressive thought made in language makes contact with another expressive thought made in language. That must occur in the local institutional setting and particular historical circumstances of a class community. Yet imagine if every class community was intent on collecting and coding shared knowledges and common experiences that emerge in the act of writing. What if this became part of the content for the nation? What if composing practices that take place in classrooms can connect to a past not codified in great books but in actual people, and imagine if these pasts were evoked to form connections between and among a new academic majority? What if an idea of the university insisted on the input of practices as they happen in nonprestigious, Hispanic Serving Institutions, like Lehman, or any other hub of innovative contact composition?

I address these questions to anyone who cares about the purpose and public good of higher education and especially to those of us who teach in the liberal arts, cultural studies, rhetorical studies, communication, literacy—those subjects of "common learnings" in "knowing and doing." The phrase "knowing and doing" was used by early-twentieth-century public educators. One Lehman College composition student used a similar phrase, "beginning again." Here she describes what happens when we write often, informally, in writing classes. That phrase depicts the work that has produced intellectual and social connections in the academy for over a century.

It is critical to reclaim this work now. Students and educators of the public university always have done, and continue to do, powerful work of a diverse democracy. We compose for shared learning and dynamic connections between self, other, and knowledge. We write back to authority and fill in the absences in liberal education curricula that leave out liberatory practices. And in our classrooms, we make contact with the real and ideal.

This project began on a lonely bus ride taken to an abandoned campus in the middle of a devastating global pandemic. I thought I could escape the chaotic world and find refuge in the familiar comforts of humanistic scholarship: reading for revelation, reporting the need for reform, and confirming belief in systems, pedagogies, core courses, and key theories. But after flying across the country and recovering forgotten archives, I ended up right back where I started: in the composition class, with students and their writing, observing this work take shape into an idea of the university whose time has come.

APPENDIX 1

DESCRIPTION OF ENGLISH 111 (COMPOSITION I)

CUNY "PATHWAYS" GENERAL EDUCATION "REQUIRED CORE," PASSED DECEMBER 1, 2011

Reports and details on English Composition in the CUNY Pathways curriculum change regularly and can be found on CUNY campus websites. In 2011 the "Core" was described as follows.

A course in this area must meet all of the following learning outcomes: A student will read and listen critically and appropriately, including identifying an argument's major assumptions and assertions and evaluating its supporting evidence. Write clearly and coherently in varied, academic formats (such as formal essays, research papers, and reports) using standard English and appropriate technology to critique and improve one's own and others' texts. Demonstrate research skills using appropriate technology, including gathering, evaluation, and synthesizing primary and secondary sources. Support a thesis with well-reasoned arguments, and communicate persuasively across a variety of contexts, purposes, audiences, and media. Formulate original ideas and relate them to the ideas of others by employing the convention of ethical attribution and citation.

Lehman College English 111 Description for select sections taught 2012–2013. Based on Lehman College Writing Council Sub-Committee Report on Composition. Report available as the Periodic Review Report.[1]

Students in English 111 will be able to:

1. Compose well-constructed essays that develop clearly defined claims, that are supported by close textual reading. To do so, students should:
    a. Write arguments to support claims in an analysis of substantive topics or text, using valid reasoning and relevant and sufficient evidence;
    b. Write informative/explanatory texts to examine and convey complex ideas and information clearly and accurately through the effective selection, organization, and analysis of content;
    c. Include narrative, when appropriate, to develop real experiences or events using effective technique, well-chosen details, and well-structured event sequences
2. Employ effective rhetorical strategies in order to persuasively present ideas and perspectives
3. Utilize terminology, methods, and various modes of analysis in her/his writing, appropriate to assignments and related readings

https://doi.org/10.7330/9781646425433.c006

4. Understand the variety of digital platforms and media available for creating texts. To do so, students should:

   a. Integrate digital media into writing, appropriate to audience, purpose, and genre
   b. Publish with digital platforms appropriate to audience, purpose, and genre

5. Apply the rules of Standard Academic English grammar

6. Adhere to academic formatting and documenting conventions of our discipline

LEHMAN COLLEGE ENGLISH 111 SECTIONS 19 AND 20 FALL 2012 FALL 2013

Textbook: Kirszner, Laurie G. ed. 2012. *The Blair Reader*. New York: Pearson.

Assignments and Grading Scale:

Narrative: 15%
Argumentative Essay 1: 15%
Argumentative Essay 2: 20%
Online Work: 10%
Attendance, Participation: 20%
Take-home midterm: 10%
Final Exam: 10%

APPENDIX 2

PHASE ONE OF RESEARCH

Coding Student Writing Archive, 2014–2018

Fall 2012: 25 students, 24 research participants. Fall 2013: 24 students, 21 participants

Artifacts: 117 Freewrites; 115 Reflective Letters

Categories Measured by the AAC&U Written Communication Values Rubric

1. Context and Purpose for Writing

2. Content development

3. Genre and Disciplinary Conventions

4. Sources and Evidence

5. Control of Syntax and Mechanics.

Coding Schema

The AACU rubric scores "level of performance" in student writing along a continuum of 1–4:

1. "benchmark" writing meets basic or introductory skill;

2–3. "milestone" writing is close to or at college-level writing;

4. "capstone" writing is at the advanced course or graduate course level.

My coding schema used a score of 1–4 to measure the frequency of mentions by students of the genres and learning outcomes required in the course:

1. does not refer to any of the genres; does not reference any of the five learning outcomes;

2–3. refers to at least one genre and at least one of the outcomes, but without explanation;

4. refers to at least one genre and at least one of the outcomes, with some explanation.

Results

177 labeled "1"

39 labeled "2 or 3"

16 labeled "4"

https://doi.org/10.7330/9781646425433.c007

APPENDIX 3

PHASE TWO RESEARCH

Coding Student Writing Archive, 2020–2022

List of phrases coded as "mentions" in freewriting samples:

* we; us; was; list of writing; gather, belongings; find a fit / fit; back writing, still; stuck; what others wanted to know, loved freewriting, was not sure

† returns; remains; circling around; translate, running; still remaining

List of phrases or terms coded as mentions in reflective letter samples:

* *you; parts in shifts; interrupted memories; still brewing; beyond / going beyond; return*

† beginning again; reach; reconsidering; come back; really together; closely reading

    * Phrases mentioned in more than half of the artifacts.
    † Phrases mentioned in 25–50 percent of the artifacts.

When phrasing was close but not identical, I list the particular phrase that evoked the most resonance among the samples. Examples of crossover mentions are detailed in chapters 3 and 4.

https://doi.org/10.7330/9781646425433.c008

NOTES

INTRODUCTION: WRITING A NEW IDEA OF THE UNIVERSITY

1. Kimiko de Freytas-Tamura, Winnie Hu, and Lindsey Rogers Cook, "It's the Death Towers: How the Bronx Became New York's Virus Hot Spot," *New York Times*, May 26, 2020, https://www.nytimes.com/2020/05/26/nyregion/bronx-coronavirus-out break.html.

2. Lehman College provides detailed descriptions of its student population by several criteria. See Lehman College, "Institutional Research Planning and Data Analytics," https://www.lehman.edu/institutional-research/interactive-factbook .php. For more on funding for CUNY during the pandemic, see New York City Public Advocate, "Addressing the Underfunding of CUNY, New York's Engine of Mobility, Innovation, and Economic Support," https://www.pubadvocate.nyc.gov /reports/addressing-underfunding-cuny-new-yorks-engine-mobility-innovation-and -economic-support.

3. CUNY political science professor Corey Robin details some of the effects of the pandemic in "The Pandemic Is the Time to Resurrect the Public University," *New Yorker*, May 7, 2020. Lehman College students offer their perspectives on the pandemic in a fall edition of the school newspaper, *The Meridian* (October 30, 2020, https://lehmanmeridian.squarespace.com/articles/october-2020/students -presidents-amp-union-reps-discuss-the-impact-of-covid-at-lehman).

4. For a summary of the curriculum reform discussions happening at this time see Flaherty (2014).

5. See Common Core State Standards Initiative, "English Language Arts Standards Introduction," https://www.thecorestandards.org/ELA-Literacy/introduction/how -to-read-the-standards.

6. See appendix 1 for a fuller description of the Pathways Common Core Structure for English Composition, passed December 1, 2011.

7. See "AAC&U Written Communication Values Rubric," https://www.aacu.org /initiatives/value-initiative/value-rubrics/value-rubrics-written-communication.

8. See appendix 1 for details about this English 111 course at Lehman College. The description of English 111 is general and there is considerable flexibility among the variety of sections offered to incoming and transfer students. However all sections must adhere to the Pathways guidelines for English Composition, which, in 2012 and 2013, included a list of outcomes. At Lehman, instructors are required to assign particular genres and to stress key competencies. In addition, Lehman English 111 students must pass an exam to move to the second level. That assessment is discussed briefly in chapter 4. It is a ninety-minute argumentative essay that makes a claim and uses evidence cited in two short articles that students receive a week prior to the exam.

9. For the first semester of research, in fall 2012, I was on a faculty fellowship (CUNY's name for sabbatical) and was not teaching. In the fall of 2013 I returned as a

full-time faculty member, teaching courses outside of composition. For both semesters of classroom research, I took leave from my position as co-coordinator of the Writing Across the Curriculum program but remained a principal investigator for our research projects.

10. See appendix 2 for details on the coding schema.

11. One example of a workshop based on this Pathways research can be found here: https://www.lehman.edu/lehman-today/provost/docs/wac-spring-rubric-work shop.pdf.

12. See appendix 3 for the pattern schema.

13. The CUNY Commons, where I blog, is https://jyood.commons.gc.cuny.edu/author /jyood. For a description of Vani Kannan's Lehman College green space project and other literacy-related activist projects discussed on the CUNY Commons, see https://www.centerforthehumanities.org/programming/activism-in-academia-iv -adjuncts-in-dialogue-action.

14. This language is taken from *The City University of New York: An Institution Adrift* (New York: Mayor's Advisory Task Force, 1999; https://cdha.cuny.edu/items/show/24 21).

15. See Gold (2008), Legg (2014), and Ostergaard and Woods (2015).

16. Almost half of the undergraduate population in America attends two-year or community colleges, and three quarters enroll at a public, nonprestige college or university. The National Center for Education Statistics tracks trends in undergraduates through the early 2000s, including the rise of "nontraditional" students. The definition of a "nontraditional" student varies across institutions, but these are the most commonly used criterion per recent data culled by the National Center for Educational Statistics ("Definitions and Data," https://nces.ed.gov/pubs/web/97578e.asp).

17. The American Academy of Arts and Sciences gathers data about undergraduate enrollment by course and degree "Most Frequently Taken College Courses" (https://www.amacad.org/humanities-indicators/higher-education/most-freq uently-taken-college-courses#31562). Studies show that close to 80 percent of colleges and universities require some form of general education. The percentage of schools that requires composition courses is slightly higher than that. See also Jaschik (2016).

CHAPTER 1: READING TO REFORM, WRITING TO FORM A WORLD SOCIETY, 1937–1945

1. The mission of Pathways is to offer "well-rounded knowledge, a critical appreciation of diverse cultural and intellectual traditions, an interest in relating the past to the complex world in which students live today, and the ability to help society create." See "About Pathways," https://www.cuny.edu/about/administration/offices /undergraduate-studies/pathways/about.

2. The phrase "world society of writers" is adopted from a review of the SLAI published by educator Lou LaBrant (1944). We return to LaBrant at the end of the chapter and to her idea that writing forms a world society.

3. To advance the "formation of democratic government" and a public life (39), reading was taught freely and especially in state-sponsored schools (Brandt 2019). In his expansive history of literacy in the United States, Carl F. Kaestle (1991) makes the point that while access to literacy remained low through the 1930s, the right and ability to read was bound up in the earliest discourse about democracy and education in America (54). Wan (2014) connects the ability to read, and other literacy skills, with how a "good citizen" was defined in American policy (37–39).

4. Originally, as Wells (2016) documents, there were seventeen "liberal arts," including familiar writing studies subjects: grammar, rhetoric, and dialectic (14). For more on the nineteenth-century scene of general education, see George P. Schmidt, *The Liberal Arts College: A Chapter in American Cultural History* (New Brunswick, NJ: Rutgers University Press, 1957). See Miller (2011) for a succinct outline of composition from the colonial era to the Harvard *Report of the Committee on Composition and Rhetoric* in 1897, especially the role that the periodical press played in the growth of college English (27–52).

5. See Menand, Reitter, and Wellmon (2017) on the general characteristics of the liberal arts and research university in the mid- to late nineteenth century (3–5).

6. Brereton (1996) finds that around ten thousand Americans studied in Germany between 1815 and 1915. The German model of specialized disciplines took hold at the end of the nineteenth century, between 1880 and 1920. Experimentation in general education picks up after this. John Guillory (2006) cites Frederick Rudolph's 1977 study, *Curriculum: A History of the American Undergraduate Course of Study since 1636*, to acknowledge the thirty-plus independent general education programs established in the 1920s and 1930s. However he ignores how these programs differed from those he describes at Harvard, Columbia, and the University of Chicago (30). See also Graff (2008, 31).

7. Davidson (2022) discusses the considerable influence that Frederick Winslow Taylor had on Eliot and other educators interested in the labor management movement (36–40).

8. For more on Eliot and composition studies, see Terrence Joseph Flaherty, *Charles W. Eliot and the Teaching of Composition* (PhD diss., Northwestern University, 1987). The elective systems spread to many universities and would influence the Experimental College at the University of Wisconsin, established in 1908. The founder of that college, Alexander Meiklejohn, defined general education as contributing to intelligence and suggested that the humanities and liberal arts colleges are the stewards of this general knowledge (G. Miller 1988).

9. Baker and Eliot were both members of the National Association of State Universities' "Committee of Ten," a group of scholars that created a list of required texts for students to read in order to be admitted to college. Applebee (1974) notes that the Committee of Ten had a "good chance" of implementing change, because committee members came from a diversity of institutions. The Committee members are listed as Albert R. Hill, president of the University of Missouri, William I. Bryan, president of Indiana University, Jacob G. Schurman, president of Cornell University, Frank Strong, chancellor of the University of Kansas, and Frank L. McVey, president of the University of North Dakota. Yet Applebee (1974) notes that the Committee's report was written in large part by Harvard's Eliot (32–33).

10. In addition to his contribution to the Committee of Ten, Butler was also involved in politics and progressive philosophy initiatives. He served as the first president of the Industrial Education Association in New York and ran for US vice president with William Howard Taft in 1912. G. Miller (1988) discusses Butler's role in Columbia's War Issues course (36–39). See also McCaughey (2003).

11. Studies of writing programs during this period also reveal experimentation in common learnings. See especially Gold (2008). Kridel (1983) is the rare example of a scholar who discusses student interest in "common learnings" but his focus is limited to the general education initiatives at Harvard.

12. Zayed (2012). Jacqueline Jones Royster (2010) traces a tradition of "flexibility" and an "ethics" of collaboration in Black colleges (377).

13. An exception to the otherwise absent federal government involvement in higher education during the late nineteenth and early twentieth centuries was the Morrill

Land-Grant Act of 1862. However, as the act expanded public school access it also enabled the federal government to occupy public land and then create institutions where the original inhabitants of that land—Indigenous peoples and then African Americans—would be excluded from admissions. See the introduction and Stein (2018).

14. See Thelin (2011, 206). In 1910 there were only ten public junior colleges; the numbers would increase steadily, especially in the 1930s. See Drury (2003) and Dougherty (1994).

15. Between World Wars I and II, as Thelin (2011) outlines, the number of students attending college would increase fivefold, with little intervention from government in terms of campus funding, admissions, graduation requirements, faculty hires or compensation, or curriculum (205–10). Hofstadter and Smith (1961) explain that even with that increase, only 5 percent of the population went to college or university at this time (477).

16. Three of the most cited books about general education point to this time and to Columbia's core courses as a primary influence. See Menand (2010), Geiger (2016), G. Miller (1988).

17. Menand (2010) argues that approaches to general education hashed out in this period led to the "two systems" we have now: core and elective (25). The University of Chicago's website references Hutchins's debates with Dewey in explaining the origins of its common core requirements. See "History of the Core," https://college.uchicago.edu/academics/core/history. Likewise, Dewey's influence is cited in the history of the core courses at Columbia University. See "The Core Curriculum," https://www.college.columbia.edu/core/oasis/history6.php. Columbia's curriculum has been the subject of many histories and memoirs, including the 1990s best-selling *Great Books*, by former *New Yorker* film critic David Denby (1997). In the conclusion, we look at a pandemic-era defense of great books (Montás 2021).

18. R. Miller (1998) astutely notes that controversy over great books courses emerged as soon as they were named potential solutions to crises in education (190–92).

19. Linguist Thomas Ricento (2003) contextualizes general education as part of a larger "Americanization" movement in the period, an effort to cultivate a "collective sense" of an American identity (611–12).

20. The Seattle Civil Rights & Labor History project chronicles the history of the KKK and offers archival history of its use of the term *Americanism* (Brianne Cook, "Watcher on the Tower and the Washington State Ku Klux Klan," http://depts.washington.edu/civilr/kkk_wot.htm). It's worth noting that a scholar with very different politics from Hutchins, the radical and anti-war historian Charles Beard, also worried about unchecked faith in Americanism. Influenced by Dewey and the Progressive Education Association (PEA) but ultimately deviating from open-discourse liberalism, Beard argued that public schools could promote social criticism and help to uncover "truths" about American history and society, such as its unequal distribution of wealth, racism, and ethnocentrism. Kazin and McCartin (2006) discuss Beard's relationship to Americanism (7), as does Jill Lepore, "In Every Dark Hour" (*New Yorker*, February 3, 2020).

21. Hofstadter and Smith (1961) record Dewey's response to Hutchins: that the central question of education must be "how far institutions can become centers of creative thought" (52). In practice, "creative thought" often ignored the traditions and contributions of nonwhite and women teachers and students. See Janie L. Nusser, "Gender's Contribution to the Rise and Fall of the Progressive Education Association, 1919–1955" (Paper presented at the Annual Meeting of the American Educational Research Association, New York: April 8–12, 1996). Fallace (2015) is informative on the issue of race and Americanism.

22.   The relationship between the progressive movement and composition is documented by Gallagher (2002) and Mastrangelo (2012). Gallagher acknowledges how this movement promoted a primarily white and male leadership and definition of literacy. Mastrangelo identifies the lesser-known feminist strands of the progressive movement. Both foreground progressivism as central to the modern discipline of composition. Neither addresses the Stanford Language Arts Investigation (University Archives, Stanford University Special Collections. 371.34 .S785 V.1: No.1–80).

23.   Kynard (2014) discusses accommodationist racism and addresses how progressive educators cooperated with admissions quotas at elite colleges and universities, many aimed at limiting access to Black, first-generation, and Jewish students (29–40). Burkholder (2007) discusses racism in progressive "intercultural" curricula of the era (96–135).

24.   Applebee (1974) makes an important point in his evaluation of this period, noting that educators evaded Dewey's civic project and relegated his work to "life adjustment" concerns. But because he looks only at one monograph, *English for Social Living*, and spends a few sentences doing so, Applebee's conclusion that the SLAI was similar to other "progressive experiments"—"lacking any principles"—is unfounded (150). Moulton (1979) addresses the SLAI as one of the "problems" of progressivism, also relying only on *English for Social Living*. Miller (2011) provides a thoughtful take on progressive-era experiments, but he too limits his research to one manuscript, *English for Social Living*, and overlooks the project's attention to public education and its relationship to common learnings (169).

25.   Richards's experiments with this curriculum would inspire the semantics movement, especially the work of Alfred Korzybski, S. I. Hayakawa, and Charles Morris. Basic English was the attempt, begun by linguist Charles Ogden of Cambridge University, to create a stable, international English language with set grammar and vocabulary, amounting to around 850 words. See Koeneke (2003) for a discussion of Richards's imperialist take on literary criticism and especially his attempt to bring Basic English to China.

26.   Leaders of the junior college movement were often presidents of elite universities seeking to promote a "social-utility" model of higher education for the working class and poor, in order to prepare students for low-wage jobs. For extensive research on the junior college movement and its classicism, see the account by rhetoric scholar William DeGenaro (2012). William H. Watkins (2001) describes the "white architects of Black education" and the progressive educators who narrowed their understanding of general education when applied to Black colleges and normal schools, believing the poor and Black graduates of these institutions could provide a ready supply of skilled manual workers (131).

27.   Kefauver was the second Dean of Education at Stanford, hired by the founding dean, Ellwood P. Cubberly (namesake of the university's library). Kefauver began his career at Columbia, researching public schools and colleges with Leonard V. Koos. The two collaborated (with several other researchers) on "The Secondary-School Population," an extensive national survey of schooling that became an important discussion point for the NCTE and cited in the *PMLA, English Journal*, and by reformers associated with the MLA and the PEA. See Dorn (2006) and Lowen (1997).

28.   The term *Americanism* traces back to the eighteenth century and referred to varieties in the language other than British. See Hansen (2006).

29.   The SLAI produced four monographs. *Foreign Languages and Cultures in American Education* (1942) lists Kaulfers, Kefauver, and Roberts as editors. Kaulfers and Roberts edit *A Cultural Basis for the Language Arts* (1937), Kaulfers edits *Modern Languages for Modern Schools* (1942), and while Roberts, Kaulfers, and Kefauver are

credited as editors of the first edition of *English for Social Living* (1943) the later editions are edited by Roberts only (1946). When I cite work authored by SLAI teacher-researchers, I use the teacher-researcher's name and the year of monograph publication. When I draw on archival material, I cite the particular Bulletin.

30.   "Public" colleges and universities as we know them now were a new phenomenon at the time. Throughout the nineteenth and early twentieth centuries, almost all higher education institutions were private (Thelin 2011). Most were chartered by religious groups or state legislators and funded by a mix of private and public sources (70–72).

31.   For a longer discussion of Flexner, see Thelin (2011, 240–42, 361–62) and Flexner (1960).

32.   While Kaulfers and Roberts, along with the teacher-researchers in the program, describe many of their students as bilingual or multilingual, there are no official records of demographics. In the case studies published in the monographs after 1937, several teachers explain that students are working, the first in their families to go to college, older than high school or junior college age, and often children of immigrants or immigrants themselves. I have tried to use the student and teacher artifacts to illuminate what I see as linguistic, racial, and cultural diversity in these SLAI classrooms.

33.   Russell (2006) discusses Burrows's research on reading but not her work on composition (249). See Reynolds (1984) for a history of freewriting that mentions Macrorie but not Burrows.

34.   *English Journal* essays detail Roberts's work on the publications and public relations committees of the NCTE (Roberts 1933). Durst (2017) links Roberts to a radical history in composition studies.

35.   For an interesting discussion of "Basic English" as it relates to Richards's legacy as a pioneer of close reading, see North (2013).

36.   In 1941, the NCTE requested that Rollins serve as a keynote speaker for an "intercultural luncheon" offered to teachers attending the annual convention in Atlanta, Georgia. However, the hotel in Atlanta did not allow this Black educator to speak to a majority-white audience. Royster (2010) looks back to this convention as inspiration for the NCTE's 1945 resolution against holding conferences in segregated states.

37.   Excerpts from reviews of the SLAI were compiled by Thornton Clark Blayne in *A Critical Appraisal of the Stanford Language Arts Investigation*. This is archived with the official bulletins. This work includes Roberts's own discussion of Rollins's work. Bulletin 35.

38.   Applebee, Langer, and Nachowitz (2011).

39.   For more about LaBrant, see Thomas (2000).

CHAPTER 2: FROM CULTURAL LITERACY
TO COMPOSITION, 1945–PRESENT

1.   See Tania D. Mitchell, "In the Wake of Multiple Pandemics," (*Liberal Education*, June 16, 2022, https://www.aacu.org/liberaleducation/articles/in-the-wake-of -multiple-pandemics).

2.   For a thorough discussion of crisis rhetoric and its relationship to curricular reform and the academy during and after the pandemic, see Cook (2021).

3.   Louis Menand, "College: The End of the Golden Age," *New York Review of Books*, October 18, 2001, https://www.nybooks.com/articles/2001/10/18/college-the-end -of-the-golden-age.

4. Newfield (2008); Smith and Bender (2008).
5. Fuller (2000) details the link between President Conant and another famous scientist and educator, Thomas Kuhn, and their shared embrace of general education and the humanities.
6. A list of critics and historians who point to *General Education in a Free Society* as central to the expansion of general education include Smith and Bender, Gary E. Miller, Louis Menand, Geoffrey Galt Harpham, Roger L Geiger, Christopher Newfield, and John Guillory.
7. By 1950, *General Education* had sold more than forty thousand copies. Much of what we know about the report comes from literary critics extolling its virtues and pointing to how it revolutionized the work of English departments in America. See Harpham (2017) and Bell (1968).
8. Bowers's *Cultural Literacy for Freedom* engages cultural literacy as it relates to the deschooling movement and informal and unstructured learning environments. For more on schools of education, teacher preparation, and cultural literacy, see Labaree (2019).
9. See especially Allan Bloom's *The Closing of the American Mind* (New York: Simon & Schuster, 1987).
10. For a discussion of Hirsch's relationship to the field of composition and an insightful take on the "rhetoricity" of *Cultural Literacy*, see Cook (2009).
11. Studies of literacy rates during the 1970s and 1980s debunk the statistics that Hirsch cites in his book and connect stories of decline in reading and writing scores to increasingly diverse schools and colleges. See Lamos (2009).
12. The general education controversy at Stanford is documented in several essays but summarized well in Alison Schneider's "Stanford Revisits the Course That Set Off the Culture Wars" (*Chronicle of Higher Education*, May 9, 1997). Linda Brodkey's *Writing Permitted in Designated Areas Only* (1996) includes an account of the culture conflict at the University of Texas, detailing the rise and fall of the composition curriculum she put in place when she was director of the writing program there. Hirsch (1987) discusses how his work was taken up by William Bennett, chair of the National Endowment for the Humanities, in the preface (xiv). See also Bennett Lovett-Graff, "Culture Wars II: A Review Essay" (*Modern Language Studies*, no. 25 [1995]: 99–124).
13. Goldie Blumenstyk, "An Author of *Academically Adrift* Strikes Again" (*Chronicle of Higher Education*, October 2, 2019, https://www.chronicle.com/newsletter/the-edge/2019-10-02).
14. Doug Lederman, "Less Academically Adrift" (*Inside Higher Ed*, May 22, 2013, https://www.insidehighered.com/news/2013/05/20/studies-challenge-findings-academically-adrift).
15. Leon Botstein, "Learning Is Like Sex: And Other Key Reasons the Liberal Arts Remain Relevant," https://www.leonbotstein.com/leon-botstein-music-room.
16. See "Written Communication Value Rubric" (Association of American Colleges and Universities, https://www.aacu.org/initiatives/value-initiative/value-rubrics/value-rubrics-written-communication).
17. Janna Anderson, Jan Lauren Boyles, and Lee Rainie, "The Future of Higher Education," Pew Research Center, July 27, 2012, https://www.pewresearch.org/internet/2012/07/27/the-future-of-higher-education.
18. The research conducted by Thaiss and Zawacki (2006) describes the "ubiquity" of terms like "evidence" and "argument" in college writing assignments (86–88). For a breakdown of the rhetorical strategies and genre conventions of writing assignments at the university level, see Melzer (2014). A discussion of the language of argument and its relationship to close reading as a methodology and ideology can be found in Murray (1991).

19. Many American institutions have engaged in general education reforms since 2010. Some examples are: the University of California, the University of Nevada, the State University of New York campuses, and the University of Florida. For a global perspective on general education reform see Joseph M. Valezano and Samuel P. Wallace, "Reforming General Education," *International Journal of Educational Reform*, Spring 2014, 98–115.

20. As of October 2022, Google Scholar tracked 1,283 citations for Carr's essay; an example of his influence in discussions of reading and cognitive science can be found in Maryanne Wolfe's popular *Proust and the Squid* (2008).

21. Thomas L. Friedman, "Come the Revolution," *New York Times*, May 5, 2012, https://www.nytimes.com/2012/05/16/opinion/friedman-come-the-revolution.html.

22. Spiros Protopsaltis and Sandy Baum, "Does Online Education Live Up to Its Promise? A Look at the Evidence and Implications for Federal Policy," https://jesperbalslev.dk/wp-content/uploads/2020/09/OnlineEd.pdf.

23. Kevin Carey, "The Creeping Capitalist Takeover of Higher Education," *Huffpost*, April 1, 2019, https://www.huffpost.com/highline/article/capitalist-takeover-college.

24. See especially Andrew Delbanco, "Endowed by Slavery," *New York Review of Books*, June 23, 2022, https://www.nybooks.com/articles/2022/06/23/endowed-by-slavery-american-universities-delbanco.

25. Christopher Newfield, "Universities after Neoliberalism," *Radical Philosophy* 2, no. 10 (Summer 2021): 77–86.

26. Andrea Lunsford and her team at Stanford conducted a five-year longitudinal study of first-year students, tracing their writing habits. See "Stanford Study of Writing" (https://swap.stanford.edu/was/20220129004722/https://ssw.stanford.edu/). One of their findings is that seeing, collecting, and valuing student writing matters as "intellectual property." A discussion of this can be found in Lunsford, Fishman, and Liew (2013). The journalist Clive Thompson (2013) has chronicled the "new literacy" and the rise in creative content that the internet enables. For a historical look at literacy and writing, see the research of linguist Dennis Baron (2009).

27. For a more thorough history of composition and its relationship to general education, see Brereton (1996), Connors (1997), Crowley (1998).

28. Project English was a more inquiry-based initiative than its 1930s predecessors, relied on the scientific principles of structuralism in linguistics, and aimed to fit into the post–World War II research-oriented English department. See chapter one for a discussion of integrated experiments promoted by the NCTE during the 1930s, especially intercultural and life-adjustment curricula.

29. Patricia Lambert Stock's *Composition's Roots in English Education* (2011, 40–44).

30. Maxine Hairston (1982) claims process as "paradigm."

31. See Perl 1995; and Donald Murray, "Teach Writing as a Process, Not Product" (*The Leaflet*, 1972, 3–6), for his list of eight features of the teaching process.

32. Peter Elbow argues that *expressivism* is not a term many process-oriented researchers claim. A reevaluation of the term is found in Elbow (2015). Elbow and Belanoff (1999) describe an approach to process as expansive, including a "variety of writing processes" that might be helpful for many kinds of "writing situations" (9).

33. For another perspective on the epistemology of this genre and the relationship between the "translingual norm" and the liberal subject, see Horner (2016).

CHAPTER 3: WRITING FOR CONTACT

1. My doctoral dissertation, completed over a decade before this classroom research, grappled with the rhetoric of process and "multiculturalism" (Lu 1994) and debated the way writing educators conjure "process" and "experience" in pedagogical imperatives. I was influenced by Spellmeyer (1996) and his understanding of experience, which Lu and Horner critique (1998).

2. "Tracking Transfer," *National Student Clearinghouse Research Center*, https://nsc researchcenter.org/tracking-transfer.

3. In the fall 2012 section of twenty-five students, eleven of us were parents or caregivers of children. Twenty worked between fifteen and thirty hours a week in addition to being full-time students.

4. For a description of how faculty at Lehman used flipped and backwards design approaches, see Gálvez and Yood (2022).

5. "Housing Insecurity and Homelessness," https://www.healthycuny.org/resources -housing-homelessness. See also "Q and A on Food Insecurity as a Barrier to Academic Success at CUNY," https://sph.cuny.edu/wp-content/uploads/2019/03 /Report_02_Food-Insecurity_Final.

6. See the 2019 report by CUNY scholars Emma Tsui et al., "A Report From: A Health Campaign for CUNY" (https://www.gc.cuny.edu/sites/default/files/2021 -05/cunyhousinginstability.pdf).

7. "Undergraduate Retention and Graduation Rates," *National Center for Educational Statistics*, May 2021, https://nces.ed.gov/programs/coe/indicator_ctr.asp.

8. "SEE Commitment to Diversity," with its attention on programs of "experiential education," focuses on extracurricular ways students can belong to various communities on campuses. See the Society for Experiential Education's August 2022 report (https://www.nsee.org/commitment-to-diversity).

CHAPTER 4: READING TO RECONSTRUCT

1. For one example of a campus reckoning with its racist and enslaving past, see Jesse James Deconto and Alan Blinder, "'Silent Sam' Confederate Statue Is Toppled at University of North Carolina," *New York Times*, August 8, 2018, https://www.nytimes .com/2018/08/21/us/unc-silent-sam-monument-toppled.html.

2. The full letter is reprinted by the media outlet *Latino Rebels* (*Latino Rebels* 2010).

3. See Melissa Castillo Planas, "Serving Students of Color at Hispanic-Serving Institutions and Beyond," January 12, 2021, https://www.latinxproject.nyu.edu/inter venxions/serving-students-of-color-at-hsi-and-beyond.

4. A description of the revised Lehman College English curriculum can be found in the Lehman College catalogue (https://www.lehman.edu/academics/undergraduate -bulletin-archive.php).

5. The CUNY Digital Archive traces student activism in the 1990s (https://cdha.cuny .edu/). The role of student activists in creating change in the American university has been well documented by historians and literacy scholars at CUNY. See especially Fabricant and Brier (2016).

6. For an extended discussion about the English department reforms, see Kannan, Walia, and Yood (forthcoming).

7. For a history of culturally responsive teaching, see Deborah A. Harmon, "Culturally Responsive Teaching through an Historical Lens" (*Interdisciplinary Journal of Teaching and Learning* 2, no. 1 [January 2012]: 12–22).

8. Chapter 2 links CUNY's Pathways to the Common Core State Standards.

9. This assignment is described in appendix 1 and again in chapter 3.

10. See the recent efforts on this at CUNY: "Free CUNY" (https://www.instagram.com/freecuny/?hl=en).

11. Lynda Barry's "The Sanctuary of School," Amy Tan's "Mother Tongue," and Bich Minh Nguyen's "The Good Immigrant Student" were essays from the course's textbook. See appendix 1 for details. These pieces were assigned early in the term, and then the class returned to them at the end of the semester. We read these essays alongside several recent newspaper and magazine reports on technology use in K–12 and college classrooms. The class related Tan and Nguyen's essays to Nicholas Carr's "Is Google Making Us Stupid?" and to essays published in the *New York Times*, such as Matt Richtel's "In Classroom of Future, Stagnant Scores" (*New York Times*, September 3, 2001, https://www.nytimes.com/2011/09/04/technology/technology-in-schools-faces-questions-on-value.html).

12. *Merriam Webster*, s.v. "content," https://www.merrian-webster.com/dictionary/content.

CONCLUSION: AN IDEA MADE IN THE PRACTICES OF THE PUBLIC

1. As the introduction discusses, required and elected writing classes are taken by the majority of the undergraduates in America.

2. The linguist and *New York Times* columnist John McWhorter joined in on the debate with "Yes, the Great Books Makes Us Better People" (*New York Times*, December 20, 2021, https://www.nytimes.com/2021/12/17/opinion/great-books-socrates.html). Brian Rosenberg, former president of Macalester College and current president in residence of the Harvard Graduate School of Education, complained that critiques like Menand's fuel the conservative right in his "This Is How the Humanities Dies" (*Chronicle of Higher Education*, January 7, 2022, https://www.chronicle.com/article/this-is-the-way-the-humanities-end). Higher education scholar and literary critic Leonard Cassuto found some common ground between Menand and Montás in "Great Books, Graduate Students, and the Value of Fun in Higher Education" (*Chronicle of Higher Education*, January 20, 2022, https://www.chronicle.com/article/great-books-graduate-students-and-the-value-of-fun-in-higher-education).

3. I wrote a letter about this, responding to Menand's essay, "The Mail" (*New Yorker*, January 24, 2022, https://www.newyorker.com/magazine/2022/01/24/letters-from-the-january-24-2022-issue). The twentieth anniversary edition of Gerald Graff's famous *Professing Literature* (2008) adds a section on the importance of writing courses in English studies.

4. Many of the histories sourced in this book are examples of expansive studies of literacy, broad understandings of the humanities, and a commons approach to academia. See Ferguson (2012), Bleich (2013), Wilder (2014), Wan (2014), Enoch and VanHaitsma (2015).

5. See the Mellon TLH website at CUNY for more information on this project (https://www.cuny.edu/academics/faculty-affairs/cuny-innovative-teaching-academy/transformative-learning-in-the-humanities/tlh-faculty-fellows/).

6. Scholars who describe the history of and problems with the first-year composition course include Nancy Welch and Tony Scott in *Composition in the Age of Austerity* (2016), David Fleming in *From Form to Meaning* (2011), and Michael Harker in *The Lure of Literacy* (2015).

7. See the scholarship of Ira Shor (1992). Dhipinder Walia and Olivia Moy, colleagues in the English department at Lehman College, initiated a student and scholar conference that promotes "activism in academia" (https://activism.commons.gc.cuny.edu/).

APPENDIX 1: DESCRIPTION OF ENGLISH 111 (COMPOSITION I)

1.   "Periodic Review Report" (https://www.lehman.cuny.edu/institutional-effective
ness/documents/2020/2014-Periodic-Review-Report.pdf).

REFERENCES

Adler-Kassner, Linda, and Elizabeth Wardle, eds. 2015. *Naming What We Know: Threshold Concepts of Writing Studies.* Logan: Utah State University Press.

Ahmed, Sara. 2012. *On Being Included.* Durham, NC: Duke University Press.

Applebee, Arthur N. 1974. *Tradition and Reform in the Teaching of English.* Urbana, IL: NCTE.

Applebee, Arthur N., Judith A. Langer, and Marc A. Nachowitz. 2010. "NCTE and the Teaching of Literature." In *Reading the Past, Writing the Future,* edited by Erica Lindemann, 173–217. Urbana, IL: NCTE.

Arum, Richard, and Josipa Roska. 2011. *Academically Adrift.* Chicago, IL: Chicago University Press.

Baron, Dennis. 2009. *A Better Pencil.* New York: Oxford University Press.

Bartholomae, David. 1995. "Writing With Teachers: A Conversation with Peter Elbow." *College Composition and Communication* 46 (1): 62–71.

Bawarshi, Anis S. 2003. *Genre and the Invention of the Writer.* Logan: Utah State University Press.

Bawarshi, Anis S. 2016. "Between Genres." In *Genre and the Performance of the Publics,* edited by Mary Jo Reiff and Anis Bawarshi, 43–40. Logan: Utah State University Press.

Bawarshi, Anis S., and Mary Jo Reiff. 2010. *Genre.* Fort Collins, CO: WAC Clearinghouse / Parlor Press.

Bazerman, Charles. 1997. "The Life of Genre, the Life in the Classroom." In *Genre and Writing,* edited by H. Ostrom Bishop, 19–26. Portsmouth, NH: Boynton/Cook.

Beaufort, Anne. 2007. *College Writing and Beyond.* Logan: Utah State University Press.

Belanoff, Pat. 2011. "Silence, Reflection, Literacy, Learning, and Teaching." *College Composition and Communication* 52 (3) 399–428.

Belanoff, Pat, Peter Elbow, and Sheryl E. Fontaine, eds. 1991. *Nothing Begins with N.* Carbondale: Southern Illinois University Press.

Bell, Derrek. 1968. *The Reforming of General Education.* New York: Columbia University Press.

Berlant, Lauren. 2009. *Cruel Optimism.* Durham, NC: Duke University Press.

Berlant, Lauren. 2022. *On the Inconvenience of Other People.* Durham, NC: Duke University Press.

Berlin, James. 1987. *Rhetoric and Reality.* Carbondale: Southern Illinois University Press.

Best, Stephen, and Sharon Marcus. 2009. "Surface Reading: An Introduction." *Representations* 108 (1): 1–21.

Bleich, David. 2013. *The Materiality of Language.* Purdue: Indiana University Press.

Bowers, C. A. 1974. *Cultural Literacy for Freedom.* New York: Elan.

Boyle, Casey. 2016. "Writing and Rhetoric and/as Posthuman Practice." *College English* 78 (6): 532–54.

Boyle, Casey. 2018. *Rhetoric as Posthuman Practice.* Columbus: Ohio State University Press.

Brandt, Deborah. 1995. "Accumulating Literacy." *College English* 57 (6): 649–68.

Brandt, Deborah. 2014. *The Rise of Writing.* Cambridge: Cambridge University Press.

Brandt, Deborah. 2019. "The Problem of Writing in Mass Education." *Utbildning & Demokrati* 28 (2): 37–53.

Brandt, Deborah. 2021. "Studying Writing Sociologically." In *The Expanding Universe of Writing Studies,* edited by Kelly Blewett, Tiane Donahue, and Cynthia Monroe, 260–70. New York: Peter Lang.

https://doi.org/10.7330/9781646425433.c009

Brereton, John C. 1996. *The Origin of Composition Studies in the American College, 1875–1925.* Pittsburgh, PA: Pittsburgh University Press.

Brim, Matt. 2020. *Poor Queer Studies.* Durham, NC: Duke University Press.

Brodkey, Linda. 1996. *Writing Permitted in Designated Areas Only.* Minneapolis: Minnesota University Press.

Bruffee, Kenneth. 1994. "Collaborative Learning and the 'Conversation of Mankind.'" *College English* 46 (7): 635–52.

Burkholder, Zoe. 2008. *Color in the Classroom.* New York: Oxford University Press.

Buurma, Rachel Sagner, and Laura Heffernan. 2020. *The Teaching Archive.* Chicago, IL: University of Chicago Press.

Burrows, Alvina Treut. 1950. "Caste System or Democracy in Teaching Reading?" *Elementary English,* no. 23, 145–48.

Burrows, Alvina Treut. 1977. "Composition: Prospect and Retrospect." In *Reading and Writing Instruction in the United States,* edited by. H. Alan Robinson, 17–43. Urbana, IL: ERIC Clearinghouse.

Burrows, Alvina Treut, Doris C. Jackson, Dorothy O. Saunders. 1939. *They All Want to Write.* New York: Library Professional Publications.

Canagarajah, A. Suresh. 2002. *A Geopolitics of Academic Writing.* Pittsburgh, PA: University of Pittsburgh Press.

Canagarajah, A. Suresh. 2012. "Autoethnography in the Study of Multilingual Writers." In *Writing Studies Research in Practice,* edited by Lee Nickoson and Mary P. Sheridan, 113–25. Carbondale: Southern Illinois University Press.

Canagarajah, Suresh. 2013. *Translingual Practice: Global Englishes and Cosmopolitan Relations.* New York: Routledge.

Carey, Kevin, 2016. *The End of College.* New York: Riverhead.

Carr, Nicholas, 2011. "Is Google Making Us Stupid?" *The Atlantic,* July/August, 2005.

Chavez, Felicia Rose. 2021. *The Anti-racist Writing Workshop.* Chicago, IL: Haymarket Books.

Chin, Elizabeth. 2016. *My Life with Things.* Durham, NC: Duke University Press.

Chuh, Kandice. 2019. *The Difference Aesthetics Makes.* Durham, NC: Duke University Press.

Conant, James Bryant. 1945. *General Education in a Free Society,* edited by James Bryant Conant. Cambridge: Harvard University Press.

Connors, Robert. 1997. *Composition-Rhetoric.* Pittsburgh, PA: Pittsburgh University Press.

Cook, Paul G. 2009. "The Rhetoricity of Cultural Literacy." *Pedagogy,* no. 9, 487–500.

Cook, Paul G. 2021. "The University of Crisis." *The American Journal of Economics and Sociology* 80 (1): 23–51.

Cresswell, Timothy. 2006. *On the Move.* New York: Routledge.

Crosby, Muriel. 1963. Foreword. In Rollins 1941, iii.

Crowley, Sharon. 1998. *Composition in the University.* Pittsburgh, PA: Pittsburgh University Press.

Cullinan, Bernice, and Lee Bennett Hopkins. 1996. "Profile: Alvina Treut Burrows." *Language Arts* 60 (4): 496–501.

Daniel, James Rushing. 2022. *Toward an Anti-Capitalist Composition.* Logan: Utah State University Press.

Davidson, Cathy N. 2022. *The New Education.* New York: Basic Books.

DeGenaro, William. 2012. "Class Consciousness and the Junior College Movement." In *Education as Civic Engagement,* edited by Gary A. Olson and Lynn Worsham, 71–94. Fort Collins, CO: Palgrave.

Delbanco, Andrew. 2012. *College: What It Was, Is, and Should Be.* Princeton, NJ: Princeton University Press.

Delpit, Lisa. 2006. *Other People's Children.* New York: The New Press.

Denby, David. 1997. *Great Books.* New York: Simon & Schuster.

Devitt, Amy J. 2016. "Uncovering Occluded Publics: Untangling Public, Personal, and Technical Spheres in Jury Deliberations." In *Genre and the Performance of Publics*, edited by Mary Jo Reiff and Anis Bawarshi, 139–56. Logan: Utah State University Press.

Dobrin, Sidney I. 2011. *Postcomposition*. Carbondale: Southern Illinois University Press.

Donahue, Christiane. 2021. "Mobile Knowledge for a Mobile Era." In *Mobility Work in Composition*, edited by Bruce Horner, Megan Faver-Hartline, Ashana Kumari, and Laura Sceniak Matravers, 17–37. Logan: Utah State University Press.

Dorn, Charles. 2006. "The World's Schoolmaster: Educational Reconstruction, Grayson Kefauver, and the Founding of Unesco, 1942–1946." *Journal of Education Society* 35 (3): 297–320.

Dorn, Charles. 2017. *For the Common Good*. Ithaca, NY: Cornell University Press.

Dougherty, Kevin James. 1944. *The Contradictory College*. Albany: SUNY Press, 1994.

Drury, Richard L. 2003. "Community Colleges in America." *Inquiry* 8 (1): 1–6.

Dryer, Dylan B. 2016. "Toward a Tactical Research Agenda on Citizens' Writing." In *Genre and the Performance of the Publics*, edited by Mary Jo Reiff and Anis Bawarshi, 60–79. Logan: Utah State University Press.

Duffy, William. 2021. *Beyond Conversation*. Logan: Utah State University Press.

Durst, Russell K, 2017. "Practical Progressivism." In *English Language Arts Research and Teaching*, edited by Russell K. Durst, George E. Newell, and James D. Marshall, 227–41. New York: Routledge.

Elbow, Peter. 1973. *Writing without Teachers*. Cambridge: Oxford University Press.

Elbow, Peter. 2012. *Vernacular Eloquence*. Cambridge: Oxford University Press.

Elbow, Peter. 2015. "'Personal Writing' and 'Expressivism' as Problem Terms." In *Critical Expressivism: Theory and Practice in the Composition Classroom*, edited by Tara Roeder and Roseanne Gatto, 15–33. Fort Collins, CO: Parlor Press.

Elbow, Peter, and Pat Belanoff. 1999. *A Community of Writers*. New York: McGraw Hill.

Enoch, Jessica, and Pamela VanHaitsma. 2015. "Archival Literacy." *College Composition and Communication* 67 (2): 216–42.

Fabricant, Michael, and Stephen Brier. 2016. *Austerity Blues*. Baltimore, MD: Johns Hopkins University Press.

Fallace, Thomas D. 2015. *Race and the Origins of Progressive Education, 1880–1889*. New York: Teachers College Press.

Felski, Rita. 2015. *The Limits of Critique*. Chicago, IL: Chicago University Press.

Ferguson, Roderick A. 2012. *The Reorder Of Things*. Minneapolis: University of Minnesota Press.

Ferguson, Roderick A. 2021. "On the Subject of Roots." *Radical Philosophy* 2 (10): 69–76.

Fitzpatrick, Kathleen. 2019. *Generous Thinking*. Baltimore, MD: Johns Hopkins University Press.

Flaherty, Colleen. 2014. "Gen Ed Worries." *Inside Higher Education*, January 3, 2014.

Fleming, David. 2011. *From Form to Meaning*. Pittsburgh, PA: Pittsburgh University Press.

Flexner, Abraham. 1960. *Abraham Flexner: An Autobiography*. New York: Simon and Schuster.

Freadman, Anne. 2012. "The Traps and Trappings of Genre Theory." *Applied Linguistics* 33 (5): 544–60.

Fuller, Steve 2000. *Thomas Kuhn: A Philosophical History of Our Times*. Chicago, IL: Chicago University Press.

Gallagher, Christopher. 2002. *Radical Departures*. Urbana, IL: NCTE.

Gàlvez, Alyshia, and Jessica Yood. 2022. "Hyflex and Teaching Fails." *The Journal of Interactive Technology and Pedagogy*, July 22, 2022. https://jitp.commons.gc.cuny.edu/hyflex-faith-and-teaching-fails-the-afterlife-of-pandemic-pedagogy.

García Peña, Lorgia. 2022. *Community as Rebellion: A Syllabus for Surviving Academia as a Woman of Color*. Chicago, IL: Haymarket Books.

Gee, James. 2014. *Literacy and Education*. New York: Routledge.

Geiger, Robert L. 1999. "The Ten Generations of American Higher Education." In *American Higher Education in the Twenty-First Century*, edited by Philip G. Altbach, Robot O. Berdahl, and Patricia J. Gumport, 61. Baltimore, MD: Johns Hopkins University Press.

Geiger, Roger L. 2016. *The History of American Higher Education*. Princeton, NJ: Princeton University Press.

Giltrow, Janet. 2002. "Meta-genre." In *The Rhetoric and Ideology of Genre*, edited by Richard Coe, Loreilei Lingard, and Tatiana Teslenko, 187–205. New York: Hampton.

Goggin, Maureen Daly. 1999. "The Tangled Roots of Literature, Speech Communication, Linguistics, Rhetoric/Composition, and Creative Writing." *Rhetoric Society Quarterly* 29 (4): 63–87.

Gold, David. 2008. *Rhetoric at the Margins*. Carbondale: Southern Illinois University Press.

Graff, Gerald. 2008. *Professing Literature*. 2nd ed. Chicago, IL: Chicago University Press.

Green, Neisha-Anne. 2016. "The Re-Education of Neisha-Anne S. Green." *Praxis* 14 (1). https://www.praxisuwc.com/green-141.

Guillory, John. 1993. *Cultural Capital*. Chicago, IL: Chicago University Press.

Guillory, John. 2006. "Who's Afraid of Marcel Proust?" In *The Humanities and the Dynamics of Inclusion since World War II*, edited by David A. Hollinger, 25–49. Baltimore, MD: Johns Hopkins University Press.

Guillory, John. 2022. *Professing Criticism*. Chicago, IL: Chicago University Press.

Hairston, Maxine. 1982. "The Winds of Change." *College Composition and Communication* 33 (1): 76–88.

Hansen, Jonathan. 2006. "True Americanism: Progressive-Era Intellectuals and the Problem of Liberal Nationalism." In *Americanism*, edited by Michael Kazin and Joseph A. McCartin, 73–89. Chapel Hill: North Carolina University Press.

Harker, Michael. 2015. *The Lure of Literacy*. Albany: SUNY Press.

Harney, Stefano, and Fred Moten. 2013. *The Undercommons*. New York: Minor Compositions.

Harpham, Geoffrey Galt. 2011. *The Humanities and the Dream of America*. Chicago, IL: Chicago University Press.

Harpham, Geoffrey Galt. 2017. *What Do You Think, Mr. Ramirez?* Chicago, IL: Chicago University Press.

Hartman, Andrew. 2016. *A War for the Soul of America*. Chicago, IL: Chicago University Press.

Harvard Committee. 1945. *General Education in a Free Society*. Cambridge, MA: Harvard University Press.

Haswell, Richard. 1991. "Bound Forms in Freewriting." In *Nothing Begins with N*, edited by Pat Belanoff, Peter Elbow, and Sheryl E. Fontaine. 32–71. Carbondale: Southern Illinois University Press.

Hayles, N. Katherine. 2001. "Limiting Metaphors and Enabling Constraints in Dawkins and Deleuze/Guattari." *SubStance* 30, no. 1–2 (94/95): 144–59.

Heller, Nathan. 2023. "The End of the English Major." *New Yorker*, February 27, 2023.

Hess, Charlotte, and Elinor Ostrom, eds. 2006. *Understanding Knowledge as a Commons*. Cambridge, MA: MIT Press.

Hinkle, Steve, and Ann Hinkle. 1990. "An Experimental Comparison of the Effects of Focused Freewriting and Other Study Strategies on Lecture Comprehension." *Teaching Philosophy* 12 (1): 31–35.

Hirsch, E. D. 1987. *Cultural Literacy: What Every American Needs to Know*. New York: Vintage.

Hofstadter, Richard, and Wilson Smith, eds. 1961. *American Higher Education*. Vol. 2. Chicago, IL: University of Chicago Press.

Holdstein, Deborah, and David Bleich. 2002. *Personal Effects*. Logan: Utah State University Press.

Hollinger, David H. 2006. Introduction to *The Humanities and the Dynamics of Inclusion since World War II*, edited by David H. Hollinger, 1–22. Baltimore, MD: Johns Hopkins University Press.

Horner, Bruce. 2016. "Reflecting the Translingual Norm." In *A Rhetoric of Reflection*, edited by Kathleen Blake Yancey, 105–24. Logan: Utah State University Press.

Horner, Bruce, Megan Faver Hartline, Ashanka Kumari, and Laura Sceniak Matravers, eds. 2021. *Mobility Work in Composition*. Logan: Utah State University Press.

Hunter, James Davison. 1992. *Culture Wars*. New York: Basic Books.

Inoue, Asao B. 2015. *Antiracist Writing Assessment Ecologies*. Fort Collins, CO: WAC Clearinghouse / Parlor Press.

Inoue, Asao B., and Tyler Richmond. 2016. "Theorizing the Reflection Practices of Female Hmong College Students." In *A Rhetoric of Reflection*, edited by Kathleen Blake Yancey, 125–46. Logan: Utah State University Press.

Jaschik, Scott. 2016. "Distribution Plus." *Inside Higher Education*, January 19, 2016.

Jung, Julie. 2011. "Reflective Writing Synecdochic Imperative." *College English* 73 (6): 628–47.

Kaestle, Carl F. 1991. *Literacy in the United States*. New Haven, CT: Yale University Press.

Kamola, Isaac, and Eli Meyerhoff. 2009. "Creating Commons." *Polygraph* 21: 5–27.

Kannan, Vani, Dhipinder Walia, and Jessica Yood. Forthcoming. "Beyond Institutional Wins." In *The Third Current of Writing at CUNY*, edited by Todd Craig, Neil Meyer, and Amy Wan. Fort Collins, CO: WAC Clearinghouse / Parlor Press.

Kaulfers, Walter V. 1942. *Modern Languages for Modern Schools*. New York: McGraw Hill.

Kaulfers, Walter V., Grayson N. Kefauver, and Holland D. Roberts. 1942. *Foreign Languages and Cultures in American Education*. New York: McGraw Hill.

Kaulfers, Walter V., and Holland D. Roberts. 1935. "Integration in Language Arts." *The School Review* 43 (10): 737–44.

Kaulfers, Walter V., and Holland D. Roberts. 1937. *A Cultural Basis for the Language Arts*. Palo Alto, CA: Stanford University Press.

Kazin, Michael, and Joseph A. McCartin, eds. 2006. *Americanism*. Chapel Hill: North Carolina University Press.

Koeneke, Rodney. 2003. *Empires of the Mind*. Stanford, CA: Stanford University Press.

Kridel, Craig. 1983, "Student Participation in General Education Reform." *The Journal of General Education* 35 (3): 154–64.

Krutch, Joseph Wood. 1954. *Is the Common Man Too Common?* Norman: University of Oklahoma Press.

Kynard, Carmen. 2014. *Vernacular Insurrections*. Albany: SUNY Press.

Labaree, David. 2019. "An Uneasy Relationship." In *Who Decides Who Becomes a Teacher*, edited by Julie Gorlewski and Eve Tuck, 68–88. New York: Routledge.

LaBrant, Lou. 1944. "Open for Inspection." *English Journal* 33 (3): 123–25.

Lamos, Steve. 2009. "Literacy Crisis and Color-Blindness: The Problematic Racial Dynamics of Mid-1970s Language and Literacy Instruction for 'High-Risk' Minority Students." *College Composition and Communication* 61 (2): 125–48.

la paperson. 2017. *A Third University Is Possible*. Minneapolis: University of Minnesota Press.

Lathan, Rhea Estelle. 2015. *Freedom Writing*. Champaign, IL: NCTE.

Latino Rebels. 2019. "Lehman College's Latinx Student Alliance Pens Letter Demanding Diversity in English Department Curriculum." *Latino Rebels*, November 21, 2019. www .latinorebels.com/2019/11/21/lehmancollegestudentletter.

Lauer, Janice. 2004. *Invention in Rhetoric and Composition*. Fort Collins, CO: WAC Clearinghouse / Parlor Press.

Legg, Emily. 2014. "Daughters of the Seminaries." *College Composition and Communication* 66 (1): 67–90.

Leonard, Lorimer Rebecca. 2021. "Managing Writing on the Move." In *Mobility Work in Composition*, edited by Bruce Horner, Megan Faver Hartline, Ashanka Kumari, and Laura Sceniak Matraers, 67–81. Logan: Utah State University Press.

Liu, Eric. 2015. "How to Be American." *Democracy* 38 (Fall). https://democracyjournal .org/magazine/38/how-to-be-american-1.

Lowen, Rebecca S. 1997. *Creating the Cold War University*. Berkeley: University of California Press.

Lu, Min-Zhan. 1994. "Professing Multiculturalism." *College Composition and Communication* 45 (4): 442–58.

Lu, Min-Zhan. 2004. "An Essay on the Work of Composition." *College Composition and Communication* 56 (1): 16–50.

Lu, Min-Zhan, and Bruce Horner. 1998. "The Problematic of Experience." *College English* 60 (3): 257–77.

Lunsford, Andrea, Jenn Fishman, and Warren Liew. 2013. "College Writing, Identification, and the Production of Intellectual Property: Voices from the Stanford Study of Writing." *College English* 75 (5): 470–92.

Mabbott, Cass. 2017. "The We Need Diverse Books Campaign and Critical Race Theory." *Library Trends* 65 (4): 508–22.

Macrorie, Ken. 1991. "The Freewriting Relationship." In Pat Belanoff, Peter Elbow, and Sheryl L. Fontaine 1991, 173–89.

Marshall, Sharon. 2009. "A Case for Private Freewriting in the Classroom." In *Writing Based Teaching*, edited by Teresa Vilardi and Mary Chang, 7–25. Albany: SUNY Press.

Mastrangelo, Lisa. 2012. *Writing a Progressive Past*. Fort Collins, CO: Parlor Press.

McCaughey, Robert A. 2003. *Stand, Columbia: A History of Columbia University in the City of New York, 1774–2004*. New York: Columbia University Press.

Melzer, Dan. 2014. *Assignments Across the Curriculum*. Logan: Utah State University Press.

Menand, Louis. 2010. *The Marketplace of Ideas*. New York: W. W. Norton and Co.

Menand, Louis. 2021. "What's So Great About Great-Books Courses?" New Yorker, December 13, 2021.

Menand, Louis, Paul Reitter, and Chad Wellmon. 2017. *The Rise of Research in the Research University*. Chicago, IL: Chicago University Press.

Miller, Carolyn. 1984. "Genre as Social Action." *Quarterly Journal of Speech* 70 (2): 151–67. http://dx.doi.org/10.1080/00335638409383686.

Miller, Carolyn. 1994. "Rhetorical Community: The Cultural Basis of Genre." In *Genre and the New Rhetoric*, edited by Aviva Freedman and Peter Medway, 67–77. London: Taylor and Francis.

Miller, Gary E. 1988. *The Meaning of General Education*. New York: Teachers College Press.

Miller, Marilyn Lee. 2003. *Pioneers and Leaders in Library Services to Youth*. Westport, CT: Libraries Unlimited.

Miller, Richard E. 1998. *As If Learning Mattered*. Ithaca: Cornell University Press.

Miller, Thomas P. 2011. *The Evolution of College English*. Pittsburgh, PA: University of Pittsburgh Press.

Montás, Roosevelt. 2021. *Rescuing Socrates*. Princeton, NJ: Princeton University Press.

Moreno-Ascenzi, Laura, and Cecilia Espinosa. 2021. *Rooted in Strength*. New York: Scholastic Professional.

Moulton, Dorothy E. 1979. "Years of Controversy in the Teaching of English." *English Journal* 68 (4): 60–66.

Murray, Heather. 1991. "Close Reading, Closed Writing." *College English* 53 (2): 195–208.

Nelson, Dana D. 2015. *Commons Democracy*. New York: Fordham University Press.

Newfield, Christopher. 2008. *Unmaking the Public University*. Cambridge, MA: Harvard University Press.

Newfield, Christopher. 2016. *The Great Mistake*. Baltimore, MD: Johns Hopkins University Press.

Newman, John Henry. 1996. *The Idea of a University*, edited by Frank M. Turner. New Haven, CT: Yale University Press.

Nordquist, Brice. 2017. *Literacy and Mobility*. New York: Routledge.

North, Joseph. 2013. "What's 'New Critical' about Close Reading?" *NLH* 44 (1): 141–57.

Noyes, Louise. 1942. "Builders Together." In *Foreign Languages and Cultures in American Education*, edited by Walter V. Kaulfers et al., 215–24. New York: McGraw Hill.

Ostergaard, Lori, and Henrietta Rix Woods, eds. 2015. *In the Archives of Composition*. Pittsburgh, PA: University of Pittsburgh Press.

Ostrom, Elinor. 1990. *Governing the Commons*. Cambridge: Cambridge University Press.

Pendleton, Charles. S. 1944. "Frontier Adventure." *English Journal* 33 (3): 125–26.

Perl, Sondra, ed. 1995 *Landmark Essays on Writing Process*. New York: Routledge.

Petraglia, Joseph. 1995. *Reconceiving Writing, Rethinking Writing Instruction*. New York: Routledge.

Plante, Blake. 2018. "The Rise of Writing: A Q&A with Deborah Brandt." National Endowment for the Humanities. https://www.neh.gov/divisions/research/featured-project/the-rise-writing-qa-deborah-brandt.

Pooley, Robert C. 1944. "All This and English Too." *English Journal* 33 (8): 236–38.

Purves, Alan C. 1988. "General Education and the Search for Common Culture," in *Cultural Literacy and the Idea of General Education*, edited by Ian Westbury and Alan C. Purves, 1–3. Chicago, IL: Chicago University Press.

Readings, Bill. 1996. *The University in Ruins*. Cambridge, MA: Harvard University Press.

Reiff, Mary Jo. 2016. "Geographies of Public Genres." In *Genre and the Performance of Publics*, edited by Mary Jo Reiff and Anis Bawarshi, 100–117. Logan: Utah State University Press.

Reiff, Mary Jo, and Anis Bawarshi. 2011. "Tracing Discursive Resources." *Written Communication* 28 (3): 312–37.

Reiff, Mary Jo, and Anis Bawarshi, eds. 2016. *Genre and the Performance of Publics*. Logan: Utah State University Press.

Reynolds, Mark. 1984. "Freewriting's Origin." *English Journal* 73 (3): 81–82.

Reynolds, Nedra. 2004. *Geographies of Writing*. Carbondale: Southern Illinois University Press.

Ricento, Thomas. 2003. "The Discursive Construction of Americanism." *Discourse & Society* 14 (5): 611–37.

Richards, I. A. 1929. *Practical Criticism*. Boston, MA: Harcourt, Brace, and World.

Richards, I. A. 1943. *Basic English and Its Uses*. London: Kagan Paul, Trench, and Co.

Richards, I. A. 1947. "The 'Future' of the Humanities in General Education." *The Journal of General Education* 1 (3): 232–37.

Roberts, Holland. D. (1933). "News and Notes." *English Journal* 3 (5): 420–22.

Roberts, Holland D. 1946. *English for Social Living*. New York: McGraw Hill.

Roberts, Holland D., and Helen Fox. 1937. "Streamlining the Forum and Debate." *English Journal* 26 (4): 275–82.

Roberts, Holland D., Walter V. Kaulfers, and Grayson N. Kefauver, eds. 1943. *English for Social Living*. New York: McGraw Hill.

Robertson, Liane, Kara Taczak, and Kathleen Blake Yancey. 2012. "Notes toward a Theory of Prior Knowledge and Its Role in College Composers' Transfer of Knowledge and Practice." *Composition Forum*, no. 26. https://compositionforum.com/issue/26/prior-knowledge-transfer.php.

Rollins, Charlemae Hill. 1941. *We Build Together: A Reader's Guide to Negro Life and Literature*. Champaign, IL: NCTE.

Rollins, Charlemae Hill. 1967. *We Build Together*. 3rd ed. Champaign, IL: NCTE.

Rollins, Charlemae Hill, and Marion Edman. 1967. "Introduction." In *We Build Together*, 3rd ed., edited by Charlemae Hill Rollins, ix–xxviii. Champaign, IL: NCTE.

Royster, Jacqueline Jones. 2010. "Savory Alliances." In *Reading the Past, Writing the Future*, edited by Erica Lindemann, 361–91. Urbana, IL: NCTE.

Rudolf, Frederick. 1962. *The American College and University*. New York: Vintage.

Rule, Hannah J. 2013. "The Difficulties of Thinking through Freewriting." *Composition Forum*, no. 27, 1–18.

Rule, Hannah J. 2019. *Situating Writing Processes.* Fort Collins, CO: WAC Clearinghouse.

Russell, David. 2006. "Historical Studies of Composition." In *Research on Composition, 1983–2003,* edited by Peter Smagorinsky, 243–63. Urbana, IL: NCTE.

Russell, Lindsay Rose. 2016. "Genre Beginnings, Genre Invention, and the Case of the English-Language Dictionary." In *Genre and the Performance of Publics,* edited by Mary Jo Reiff and Anis Bawarshi, 84–99. Logan: Utah State University Press.

Scott, Fred Newton. 1913. "Our Problems." *English Journal* 2 (1): 1–10.

Sedgwick, Eve Kosofsky. 1997. *Novel Gazing.* Durham, NC: Duke University Press.

Shipka, Jody. 2011. *Towards a Composition Made Whole.* Pittsburgh, PA: University of Pittsburgh Press.

Shor, Ira. 1992. *Culture Wars.* Chicago, IL: Chicago University Press.

Smith, Wilson, and Thomas Bender, eds. 2008. *American Higher Education Transformed, 1940–2005.* Baltimore, MD: Johns Hopkins University Press.

Snyder, Thomas D, ed. 1992. *120 Years of American Education.* Washington, DC: National Center for Education Statistics.

Spahr, Juliana. 2001. *Everybody's Autonomy.* Tuscaloosa: Alabama University Press.

Spellmeyer, Kurt. 1996. "After Theory." *College English* 58 (8): 893–913.

Spratt, Danielle, and Bridget Draxler. 2019. "Pride and Presentism." *MLA Profession.* https://profession.mla.org/pride-and-presentism-on-the-necessity-of-the-public-humanities-for-literary-historians.

Stein, Sharon. 2018. "Confronting the Racial-Colonial Foundations of US Higher Education." *Journal for the Study of Postsecondary and Tertiary Education,* no. 3, 885–86.

Sternglass, Marilyn. 1997. *Time to Know Them.* New York: Routledge.

Stock, Patricia Lambert, ed. 2011. *Composition's Roots in English Education.* Portsmouth, NH: Heinemann.

Taczak, Kara, and Liane Robertson. 2016. "Reiterative Reflection in the Twenty-First Century Writing Classroom." In *A Rhetoric of Reflection,* edited by Kathleen Blake Yancey, 42–63. Logan: Utah State University Press.

Thaiss, Chris, and Terry Zawacki. 2006. *Engaged Writers and Dynamic Disciplines.* New York: Heinemann.

Tharp, James B. 1939. "Foreign Languages and the Social Studies." *The Modern Language Journal* 23 (4): 301–3.

Tharp, James B. 1946. "Reviewed Works." *Educational Research Bulletin* 25 (1): 23–24.

Thelin, John. 2011. *A History of Higher Education.* Baltimore, MD: Johns Hopkins University Press.

Thomas, P. L. 2000. "Blueprints or Houses? Lou La Brant and the Writing Debate." *English Journal* 89 (3): 85–89.

Thompson, Clive. 2013. *Smarter Than You Think.* New York: Penguin.

Tobin, Lad. 2011. "Process Pedagogy." In *A Guide to Composition Pedagogies,* edited by Gary Tate, Amy Rupiper, and Kurt Schick, 1–18. Cambridge: Oxford University Press.

Trimbur, John. 1989. "Consensus and Difference in Collaborative Learning." *College English* 51 (6): 602–16.

Turner, Frank M. 1996. "Newman's University and Ours." In *The Idea of a University,* 282–302. New Haven, CT: Yale University Press.

Turner, Tilley Glennett. 1999. *Follow in Their Footsteps.* New York: Puffin Books.

United States Bureau of Education (USBE), Committee of the National Council of Education. *Economy of Time in Education* 38. Washington, DC: Government Printing Office, 1913.

Villanueva, Victor, ed. 2003. *Cross-talk in Comp Theory.* Champaign, IL: NCTE.

Wan, Amy. 2014. *Producing Good Citizens.* Pittsburgh, PA: Pittsburgh University Press.

Wardle Elizabeth. 2009. " 'Mutt Genres' and the Goal of FYC." *College Composition and Communication* 60 (4): 765–89.

Warner, Michael. 2002. *Publics and Counterpublics.* Brooklyn, NY: Zone Books.

Watkins, William H. 2011. *The White Architects of Black Education.* New York: Teachers College Press.

Weinstein, Arnold. 2021. *The Lives of Literature.* Princeton, NJ: Princeton University Press.

Welch, Nancy, and Tony Scott. 2016. *Composition in the Age of Austerity.* Logan: Utah State University Press.

Wells, Cynthia A. 2016. "Realizing General Education: Reconsidering Conceptions and Renewing Practice." *ASHE Higher Education Report* 42 (2): 1–85. https://doi.org/10.1002/aehe.20068.

Wilder, Craig Steven. 2014. *Ebony and Ivy.* London: Bloomsbury Publishing.

Wilson, Herbert B. 1973. *Cultural Literacy Laboratory.* McGill Journal of Education. https://files.eric.ed.gov/fulltext/ED087698.pdf.

Wolfe, Maryanne. 2008. *Proust and the Squid.* New York: Harper.

Yancey, Kathleen Blake. 1998. *Reflection in the Writing Classroom.* Logan: Utah State University Press.

Yancey, Kathleen Blake, ed. 2016. *A Rhetoric of Reflection.* Logan: Utah State University Press.

Zayed, Kevin S. 2012. "Reform in the General Education Movement: The Case of Michigan State College, 1938–1952." *The Journal of General Education* 61 (2): 141–75.

INDEX

ABOUT THE AUTHOR

Jessica Yood is professor of English at the City University of New York, Lehman College and the Graduate Center, teaching courses in writing, contemporary literature, and rhetoric. A former coordinator of the Writing Across the Curriculum program and a recent fellow in the Mellon Foundation's Transformative Learning in the Humanities program, Yood is active in literacy advocacy and public humanities projects. In 2015 she was named Teacher of the Year. Yood writes about culture, composition, and the history of American higher education, and her work can be found in *Inside Higher Education* and in a variety of scholarly journals.